How to Retire in Thailand

& Double Your Income

by

Godfree Roberts, Ed.D.

Copyright © 2012 Godfree Roberts
www.thailandretirementhelpers.com

ISBN: 978-1470138721

All rights reserved. Published 2013.

Printed in the United States of America

Publisher's address:
10336 Loch Lomond Rd.
Middletown, CA 95461

LIVING ON SOCIAL SECURITY

If you're a fellow victim of the financial crisis you know that life has handed us a lemon right at the end of our working lives. The trick is how to make lemonade out of it?

I've found that it's completely possible to live in comfort and beauty on $1,200 a month – something I imagined would be impossible when I was expelled from the middle-class five years ago.

(I grew up in Australia, lived in Japan, then got my doctorate at UMass, Amherst. I married, started a California company and lived an enjoyable life, including annual visits to Paris. The financial crisis wiped me out, and I'm now 73 years old and enjoying life more than ever – to my great surprise.)

In Thailand my $1200/mo. Social Security check allowed me to rejoin the middle class. This book explains in detail exactly what it took – and what it takes – to live comfortably on that income, on half that income, and on twice that income. It's packed with budgetary details, and loads of practical stuff like Thai dental care, food costs, and the availability of medical insurance.

See you in Thailand,

Godfree Roberts,
www.thailandretirementhelpers.com

Chiang Mai
April 2013

MY FIRST LETTER HOME

Dear Folks,

Two months ago I moved into a working class part of town to be near Thai friends. Living here on the wrong side of the tracks has been educational. For some reason it brought to mind my former life in Beverly Hills.

Far from being the earthly paradise that I had expected, Beverly Hills resembled Forest Lawn cemetery: manicured, quiet, and dead. Not merely dead in that nobody was ever seen walking on the manicured sidewalks. Not dead in the sense of zero interaction between residents: most interaction was actually negative. Make too much noise or let a party run too late and a "neighbor" would literally be at your gate the next morning to serve you with a lawsuit.

My present neighborhood is about as far from Beverly Hills as neighborhoods can get, socially, culturally, and geographically.

As I write, there's a karaoke party going on in the carport (most things here, from family reunions to parties to businesses of all kinds, happen in carports).

As I came up the stairs earlier this evening my neighbors, for the umpteenth time, begged me to join them for dinner--or at least a drink. They are relentless in their hospitality.

Tonight, once the music ends, the fireworks will start. Fireworks, like most things in Thailand, are unregulated, and the most popular ones sound like artillery shells exploding above your head or, tonight, outside my window.

Oddly enough, the fireworks don't upset the dozen dogs that live on my block. Though much loved, they are allowed to run (and breed) freely. And to bark whenever, and for as long as, it amuses them. Thai dogs have a great sense of humor, so that's a lot of barking. In fact, I plan to do a video of the hilarious synchronized barking competitions that regularly go on across the street from me.

Tonight's party is in reaction to a neighborhood incident that gave me a glimpse into working-class Thai communal life.

Education is relatively new here and compulsory schooling only goes to age 14. A neighborhood boy was therefore a local celebrity when he became not only the first in his family to attend University, but the first in the entire neighborhood of 15,000 people. Everyone took great pride in his progress especially his father, a road worker, who invited the entire community to attend his graduation from engineering school tomorrow.

The boy was killed last night in a motorcycle accident which led to open tears throughout the neighborhood today and a spontaneous Buddhist ceremony earlier this evening which shut down traffic as people brought plastic chairs to sit in and flowers and gifts to console the desolate parents. It was lovely

to see: with no public spaces, the flowers
blanketed the road.

So, tonight we dance...

WHY LIVE ABROAD?

Before we get to Thailand, let's look at the big picture. Getting out of the house is always a relief. Getting out of the country is positively therapeutic. Here are twenty reasons to live abroad:

1. You don't have to dream about traveling any more. You're there.
2. You don't have to say the same things to the same people every day.
3. You can effectively double your income. Your dollar buys 2-3 times more.
4. You start a whole new life. Literally, a "fresh start".
5. You become a minimalist, paring your life to essentials.
6. You're a novelty. Your mere presence causes children to run and hide.
7. You gain daily insights into human nature. Especially yours.
8. You abandon your baggage. Old habits and attitudes just evaporate.
9. You don't know what will happen once you get up in the morning.
10. You'll be more broad-minded and compassionate.
11. Every breeze will smell new, every flavor taste fresh, every sound: different.
12. You'll experience a rush of creativity and new ideas.
13. You'll be functionally illiterate: as vulnerable as a child again.
14. You feel energy you haven't experienced since you were 20.
15. You see new opportunities everywhere.
16. You meet adventurous, interesting people. You'll be one of them.
17. You'll be exposed to ideas you'd never encounter in ordinary life.
18. You can invite friends to visit you in your adopted country.
19. Old friends will be envious and want to hear your adventures.
20. You'll appreciate your home country much, much more.

WILL YOU LIKE THAILAND?

There's no way to know until you get here, of course. But there are some important "likes" to consider. If enough of them seem important to you then perhaps they will outweigh the "dislikes" that come with every person and place. I cover the dislikable aspects in the final chapter of this book, *The Downside*.

The Secret of Life
Westerners are always searching for happiness, mostly by indulging in money, food and sex. Thais like those things too, but their culture helps them to not depend upon outside stimuli to distract them from happiness. Thais know the secret of life: there's nothing we can do to *become* happy; we can only *be* happy.

The Best Country on Earth?
Let's see what other expatriates who have lived all over the world have to say about *their* favorite countries. Each year Hong Kong Shanghai Bank (HSBC) conducts a survey of 3,000 expatriates

around the world to discover the best countries for foreigners to live in. Out of 110 countries considered, 31 stood out. Here's how Thailand ranks in each criterion against the other 30:

Overall: **#1**
Finding accommodation: **#1**
Organizing healthcare: **#1**
Working environment: **#2**
Healthcare access and quality: **#2**
Quality of accommodation: **#3**
Schools for children: **#3**
Work / life balance: **#3**
Healthy diet: **#4**
Traveling more: **#5**
Organizing finances: **#6**
Enjoying local food: **#7**
Entertainment: **#8**
Making friends: **#9**
Local transport: **#10**
Social life: **#10**
Sports: **#10**
Fitting in the new culture: **#11**
Integrating into the community: **#11**
Local weather: **#11**
Local work culture: **#11**
Setting up utilities: **#12**
Commuting: **#13**
Local shops and markets: **#13**
Using the local language: **#13**
Local culture: **#15**
Getting used to local food: **#17**
Making local friends: #17
Learning the local language: **#25**

So it's not just my imagination. Thousands of experts agree: if you're going to live abroad, Thailand is the best country on earth to live. Here are some 40 unconventional reasons (plus a bonus) for spending extended time in Thailand. Take your pick of what matters most to you:

Forty Reasons to Live in Thailand

1. Culture: It has taken Thais 1500 years to create a culture devoted to happiness, tolerance, and beauty. As guests there, all we have to do is enjoy it.

2. Cost of Living: If you live on a fixed income, you can more than double its buying power just by moving here.

3. Climate: Some like it hot, and Thai summers oblige. Some like it warm, Thai winters are wonderful. And there are always the cool mountains and 1,000 km of white, sandy beaches. The average temperature in Chiang Mai, where I live, is 77 F (25C).

4. Thai Women: Beautiful, gentle, gracious, and charming. They're hard to beat.

5. Beaches: Sure, other countries have beaches, but the hundreds of miles of beaches here are attached to Thailand!

6. **Beer**: Something for every palate: Singha, Leo, Chang, Tiger, Phuket, Klassik, the list goes on. Served *over ice.*

7. **Martial arts**: Unique, fast-moving, Muay Thai draws enthusiasts from around the world.

8. Flowers: Orchids grow wild everywhere. And orchids are just the beginning of Thailand's floral glory. You could spend a lifetime on the flowers alone.

9. Jungles: Thailand's jungles are fascinating: filled with flowers, animals, and exotic tribal people, all within a day's walk of bars serving cold beer.

10. Ethnic Diversity: Thailand is home to a wonderful variety of peoples each with a unique language, history, cuisine, costume, and sense of humor. A lifetime's study and delight.

11. Nursing, Medical and Dental Care: Millions of people come to Thailand just because of the quality (and cost) of its medical care.

12. Shopping: From banana leaves spread out on the pavement at dawn to gigantic, European hypermarkets, Thailand offers an unparalleled variety of inexpensive shopping experiences.

13. **Smiles**: Thais' smiles came 1,000 years before the tourist slogan (*The Land of Smiles*). The tourists might leave but the smiles won't.

14. **Night Life**: If you like your fireworks at 2 a.m., dancing, singing, music cold beer and cheap whisky, Thailand is heaven.

15. Safety: Women and children can walk the streets more safely here, day or night, than almost any place on earth.

16. History: Never colonized, so no 'attitude' towards foreigners. A unique and wildly divergent amalgam of myth, legend, and cultures, Thai history offers lifetimes of study.

17. Festivals: Like dressing up? Blowing things up? Setting things on fire? Singing? Dancing? Rowing? Looking at flowers? Dousing people with water? Thailand has a festival just for you. As I was coming to work this morning traffic was held up for miles to make room for a gigantic, wild-looking dragon snaking down the middle of the highway. Thousands of people will be late for work. Great!

18. Restaurants and Speakeasies: They're literally *everywhere*: in carports, under houses, on vacant lots, in alleys, streets, on rivers, mountains, in temples. And every one has her own idea of how to prepare food. Nobody cooks at home here. Want to sell whisky by the roadside? Go ahead! No permit needed. No zoning, either.

19. **Things to Do**: From hot springs to transvestite night clubs, Thais find room in their hearts, minds, wallets, and schedules for just about every form of human diversion.

21. **Animism + Hinduism + Buddhism + Christianity + Confucianism?** Thais *add* new religions to their existing ones. And there's room in Thailand for *all* of them. Even mixed together in one person! Talk about tolerance.

22. **The weather**: T-shirt, shorts, flip-flops all year round. When the temperature drops below 70F Thais bundle up and enjoy shivering.

23. **Tipping:** Taxi drivers are ecstatically happy with a 30 cent tip. When I tip my breakfast server 15¢ she smiles delightedly and bows (the *wai*) deeply.

24. **World's most varied coffee shops**: Riverside? Mountain top? Local coffee? Transvestite coffee shops serving imported organic coffee? We've got you covered.

25. **Store clerks *wai* you for buying a carton of milk:** Transactions begin and end with a bow and a blessing. What's not to like about that?

26. **Noodle carts are part of the traffic flow**: Five lanes of rush hour traffic + one guy pushing a noodle cart, at night, without lights? No problem!

27. **Entertainment**: Cable TV has 6 English-language channels, plus German, French, Vietnamese and Chinese. There are movieplexes, festivals, and holidays, including one (*Loy Krathong*) devoted to setting things on fire and floating them into the sky!

28. **"Traffic"** is an excuse for anything: Thais' politeness is matched only by their lack of punctuality. That's why "traffic" is so handy.

29. **You're More Interesting than an Elephant**: In many parts of Thailand children will literally topple over as they watch you go by– while scarcely noticing an elephant. Finally, you're getting the attention you deserve.

30. **The Language**: Written Thai is not an alphabet and spoken Thai depends on tones as much as on syllables. Learning it opens a new window on the world–and parts of your brain.

31. **Fresh Mango with Sticky Rice**: Thailand's gift to civilization. Fall in love with food all over again...for 60¢.

32. **Temples on Every Block**: Sometimes two or three. And talk about exotic! You can sit and boggle for hours. I see a new one-- always unique--every few days.

33. **Thai Women:** They *really* forgive and forget. Heartbreak? Disappointment? Betrayal? Thai women can (after the initial knife-wielding onslaught) just drop it completely and move on.

34. **Transportation:** Limo? Air train? Taxi? Pedicab? *Tuktuk? Songtaew?* Canoe? Bus? Plane? Train? Scooter? You name it, it's affordable and it's waiting for you.

35. **Accommodation:** Modern Thai houses are cool, sturdy, and airy. Traditional ones are beautiful and built of rosewood and teak. And cheap.

36. **Fighting:** Cock-fights, cricket fights, kite fights, guy-fights, gal-fights, mud-fights and the foreigners' favorite: bar-fights. Yep, we've got you covered.

37. **Freedom**: Seriously, you're free to do almost anything you can think of so long as you don't harm anyone else. In Thailand, you'll discover what "unregulated" really means!

38. **Happy**, **Laughing Drunks**: Fights are rare and usually confined to foreigners. Laughs are plentiful. Most nights, people sit around outdoors drinking beer but, apart from a lot of giggling and singing, that's about it.

39. **Wonderful drivers**: Regardless of freaked-out foreigners' opinions, you'll find that Thais are *extremely* considerate, patient, and skilled.

40. **Therapy**: Thailand is so exotic, so different, and so beautiful that it literally re-sets our minds, bodies, and hearts. It takes us out of ourselves and our concerns and allows us "time out" to reconsider life.

41. **(Bonus) Alzheimer's Prevention.** Living in Thailand makes you use your mind every day and builds your memory. You'll have to remember places and landmarks (maps and addresses are not very useful), new words, a new alphabet, and new meanings, customs, customs, money, and faces, foods...

Know Thyself: Will Thailand Suit You?

Living in a tropical paradise sounds great but I've met expats who are unhappy in Thailand and spend hours every day on expat blog sites spreading their misery with snide comments about Thailand and the Thais. I suspect they weren't happy back home, either, but nevertheless it's important to be realistic about what it takes to live in a foreign country with a different culture, climate, and level of development.

There are two phases to this consideration: personal and practical. The personal phase costs nothing and should come first. If you're not personally suited to living in Thailand then knowing that can save you a lot of time and trouble.

Self-Evaluation for Life in Thailand

In this phase you systematically identify your own values and rank them in order of importance. Then–ideally with a close friend or two–see how well your profile matches expatriate life.

We typically value emotional states of being. We use possessions and relationships to *attain* those emotional states. What emotional states do you want to feel most days? Healthy? Loved? Excited? Admired? Secured? Certainty? Variety? Significance? Growing? Successful? Here's a simple method for finding out.

1. **Take a look** at this list of personal values. Pick six that are most important to you and rank them–without thinking too much–in order of their importance:

    Accomplishment
    Adventure
    Beauty
    Calm, quietude, peace
    Challenge
    Change
    Cleanliness, orderliness
    Communication
    Community
    Continuous improvement
    Delight of being, joy, happiness
    Discovery
    Diversity
    Enjoyment
    Family
    Freedom, Liberty
    Friendship
    Fun
    Global view
    Health
    Individuality
    Inner peace, calm, quietude
    Knowledge
    Love, Romance
    Money
    Openness
    Other's point of view, inputs
    Personal Growth
    Pleasure
    Safety
    Security
    Service
    Spirit, Spirituality in life
    Stability
    Tolerance

Tradition
Tranquility
Variety
Well-being
Wisdom

Here's the list I made of the states I value:
1. Delight of being, joy, happiness
2. Discovery
3. Global view
4. Health
5. Knowledge
6. Wisdom

2. **Take your first choice**, (for me it is 'Delight of being') and contrast it to each of the others, one at a time, slowly and deliberately.

Do I really value Delight...more than Discovery? For me they are the same thing.
More than a Global view? Again, I delight in having my perspective widened by exposure to different cultures, so they're the same thing;

More than Health? No. To be honest, there's not much I won't do to improve my health. I eat a healthy diet, don't smoke or drink, do yoga regularly, etc. I cannot imagine being delighted about *anything* if I weren't healthy. So, because my entire lifestyle is obviously centered on health, I move Health up to #1, and continue the process.

3. **Continue ranking them in importance** by selecting those you can't you do without and are least willing to compromise on.

4. **Ask yourself** "How do I *get to* my #1 choice each day?" *What do you do to attain it*? For me it's regular exercise and diet every day for the past 45 years. If security is #1 for you, how to you *get* there? By knowing what's going on around you at all times? By be able to pay your bills effortlessly? By carrying a gun? Etc.

5. **What drives you?** Looking back, what has driven you to do the things you did, and to become the person you are in the situation you're now in? Was it always, for example, an insistence on a certain lifestyle–always with the same crowd, always in the same surroundings, with a predictable daily routine? You may have fantasized about living adventurously, but that's not the evidence of your life.

6. **Evaluate**. Here's where good friends come in. Show them your list and ask if your profile choices match their impression of you. If you've put Adventure high on your list but confined your adventurousness to Disneyland, then notice that evidence. Your friends certainly will. They'll invariably have some interesting observations and, of course, seize the opportunity to rib you about moments in your life you would prefer to forget. I recommend you begin this discussion when everyone is on their second beer–especially you.

7. **Make an informed decision**. You're free to disregard the results. But you've informed yourself before you start spending time and money. Even if you move to Phase 2 then decide that expat life is not for you, you'll know why and feel much clearer about your decision.

Evaluate Life *in* Thailand

If you like the idea of living in Thailand, plan to spend at least a month actually *living* here. I recommend spending a fortnight in an urban environment like Chiang Mai, and a fortnight on idyllic Koh Chang Island (or a semi-rural equivalent like Chiang Rai). Two weeks in each location will give you time to study the people, culture, and the Thai environment.

Then you'll know yourself and you'll know what it's like to live in Thailand. So you can make a fully informed decision. If you decide that Thailand is for you I hope you'll take our workshop. We'll plug you into the Land of Smiles so that you can begin your new life immediately, instead of floundering around for a year and wasting precious money like I and thousands of others did.

Regardless of whether or not you take the workshop, feel free to contact me any time for help. I actually enjoy it. (Maybe I should have put that on my 'values' list...).

Thais' Own Evaluation of Their Lives

Below you can see the result of an international poll conducted by the Gallup Organization to find out how much different nationalities are suffering. Just so you don't have to take only *my* word for it!

Countries Where "Suffering" Was Lowest in 2011

	Suffering
Brazil	<1%
Thailand	1%
Canada	1%
Luxembourg	1%
Netherlands	1%
United Arab Emirates	1%
Denmark	2%
Australia	2%
Saudi Arabia	2%
Oman	2%
New Zealand	2%
Turkmenistan	2%
Sweden	2%
Zambia	2%
Somaliland region	3%
Israel	3%
Austria	3%
Finland	3%
Kuwait	3%
Panama	3%
United States	3%
Congo (Kinshasa)	3%
Qatar	3%
Mongolia	3%

GALLUP

Any Regrets?–Video

I asked some friends if they have any regrets about retiring to Thailand?

Here's the video of their response.

Have a question about this chapter? A suggestion?
Email me: **godfree@thailandretirementhelpers.com**
I'll get back to you within 48 hours.

THAI CULTURE

The Village Girl
(A recent letter home)

A British friend is married to a charming Thai woman who once told me her life story.

Lek was born in a small, poor, remote village in Northern Thailand near the Myanmar (Burma) border. When she was 5 her parents were killed in a bus accident and she and her little brother were orphaned, without traceable relatives.

The village raised both children and when Lek consistently came top of the class in the nearby primary school, they paid for her to complete her secondary education. She was only the third villager ever to complete high school, where she again excelled.

During the last semester her high school principal suggested to the village elders that they consider sending her to university. Since none of them knew what a university was it took several meetings before they agreed.

With a partial tuition scholarship from the government and a monthly pledge of money from each village family it was arranged that she would study at Chiang Mai University. It meant that she would leave her village for the first time and live at the university.

The villagers understood that she would need money for food and clothes and again pledged their collective support. Having no idea of the cost of living in a city they created an allowance for her that would have been sufficient for a young person living in the village: 3000 Baht per month--$75 at the time.

Lek tells hilarious stories about arriving on campus--itself far larger than her home village--and her first realization that on her allowance she would starve to death, go without clothes, or be unable to purchase paper and pencils.

Her solution to the last problem was to condense her notes from each one-hour lecture into a single line of tiny writing and then rely on her tenacious memory.

She solved the other two problems in a single blow: her only extracurricular activity was the university's drama club which kept an extensive wardrobe from previous years' productions.

On laundry days, when her only college outfit was in the wash, Lek would appear at lectures dressed sometimes as a Dutch farm girl...or a hooker, blithely explaining that she was preparing for a play and getting into character. She thus developed a reputation for being an eccentric, free-spirited type which, she says, was entirely undeserved.

The hooker's outfits came in doubly useful since, when her money was running low she would cruise the local bars in the early evenings before business picked up, saunter in, and scrounge peanuts, crackers or snacks from the bar. She says she was so scrawny that she was surprised that anyone believed her act but later found that all of the barkeepers (mostly women in Thailand) had been tipped off by fellow students and would keep the best snacks aside for her arrival. After graduation she married my friend, her former professor, and now runs her own business.

Her husband later told me the sequel to her story. He regularly receives requests for money from her village. The villagers have never asked for anything for themselves in return for their years of sacrifice. All they have ever requested is help in maintaining the little Buddhist temple that occupies the most prominent and beautiful hilltop in the village.

The People

If you don't like a country's people you probably won't like the country. Maybe to visit, but certainly not to live. So here's a brief profile of an ancient people, mostly from the Tai tribe, who migrated from China many centuries ago,

Thais are the only culture I've encountered who always know what it is to look and feel and act and be completely happy. That's the foundation of everything they do. Do they always succeed? Of course not; but lapses are relatively rare. They understand that happiness isn't something you *find* in the world. Happiness is what you *bring* to the world.

We Westerners imagine that if we change our feelings then we will be happy. Thais know that feelings *follow* their actions: if they *act* happy, they'll soon *feel* happy. Put another way, they understand that the way you *seem* is the way you *are*. We may not be able to control our feelings, but we can control our actions.

I'll mentions this again later in the book because it really is the key to appreciating Thailand. If you want to study the art of being happy, Thailand is a good place to start.

Thai Culture

When Westerners hear the word "culture" we tend to think of museums, art galleries, and concerts. But the word itself is derived from the Latin *cultus*, 'worship', 'cultivated', 'care', 'cultivation'. The Thais are a cultivated people. They've spent a thousand years cultivating happiness. In order to make it real they also study and practice tolerance and cooperation. Because cooperation + tolerance = peace. Without cooperation and peace, happiness is hard to sustain.

Off the top of your head, can you think of another society of 60 million tolerant, cooperative, happy people? I ask because a surprising number of Westerners who settle here loudly proclaim that the Thais' happiness is 'fake', thereby justifying their own grumbling and un-happiness. They don't understand that happiness is a discipline that requires practice, not just something that happens when you win the lottery.

Beauty

It's possible to be happy if you're surrounded by ugliness but it's hard work. So the sensible Thais surround themselves with beauty.

For starters, they chose a country with the most fertile soil on earth, 2,000 kilometers of mighty forests, white coral beaches and islands, fog-drenched mountains and legendary rivers. Within the forests live some of the most exotic people and the most unforgettable animals on earth. The soil, rivers, and sun produce rice and other crops in abundance. Wait 'til you see the fruit and, more important, taste it. I'm not fruit eater but I can't resist Thai fruit because it tastes so darn good.

To the natural beauty Thais have added their own love of personal beauty: graceful bodies and clothing, exotic buildings, paintings, music, dance. Not just as afterthoughts, but as the major focus of everyday life. Not just here and there but everywhere, every day.

Art and Music

This is just a brief mention of Thailand's thriving art and music scene. Seeing is believing, so I'll wait 'til you get here to introduce you to the local scene. In the meantime, here's a local Chiang Mai artist you might want to get to know, Pakitsilp Varamissara, whose work always delights me.

His light-hearted fusion of ancient Northern Thai (the northern, Lanna, Kingdom was only united with the southern part of the country in the 1930s) with French Impressionism is constantly fresh, as you can see in his muralist paintings.

He's part of a thriving art scene which is intensified by the fact that almost every artist on earth comes to visit and to be inspired by Thailand's unique aesthetic.

And music? On any evening you can sit by the river in an antique bar, sip $2 cold beers, and listen to Thailand's greatest traditional musicians. Stay all night, it's hypnotic.

The Best Thai Movies—With Subtitles

Thai movies are an easy way to get acquainted with Thailand, its culture and its language. Start by looking for these DVDs on Netflix. There's no easier or more enjoyable way to study Thai language and culture than to watch a classic Thai movie. Here are eight of the best, all with English subtitles:

Ong Bak: ***Muay Thai Warrior***. An action film with Tony Jaa as a young villager trying to recover a stolen Buddha head. This film enjoyed great popularity in the west and Tony Jaa became a major worldwide celebrity.

Ong Bak 2 and Ong Bak 3: Success breeds sequels or, in this case, prequels. Both of these films take Tony Jaa's character back to the 15th. Century when magic was still alive and well. In addition to being enjoyable, well-produced films they give a rich depiction of medieval Thailand--at least as the filmmakers imagined it. Both showcase Tony Jaa as actor and director, enhanced by much bigger budgets.

A Man Called Tone: A sophisticated film with a strong script, fascinating characters, and some of the best acting ever seen in Thai cinema. Thai critics and intellectuals hailed it as proof that Thailand could produce great movies.

The Protector: Another Tony Jaa vehicle: adrenaline-pumping, and high octane Thai movie also starring Tony Jaa. All action, all the time, it is nevertheless both fun to watch and a useful lesson in Thai slang.

Monrak Looktung: ***Magical Love in the Countryside***. A charming musical was made in 1970 and remade in 2005. A rural love story packed with Thai 'peasant' tunes. Many consider this the high point of 20th. Century Thai filmmaking. It ran for over 6 months in theaters throughout Thailand and adds yet another dimension to our appreciation of Thai culture.

Tropical Malady: A romantic double tale of gay love. It was the first Thai film to win the coveted Jury Prize at the Cannes Film

Festival. At first it was ignored but Quentin Tarantino's advocacy of it forced critics to take a second, closer look.

Kao Cheu Karn: Thailand's first great advocacy film: it forced the elite and the middle class to take an unflinching look at Thailand's hidden (feudal) problems of corruption and poverty. Its impact on Thai society and, subsequently, politics was staggering and persists to this day.

Getting Along

Because my background is in education I meet regularly with graduate students of Education at Chiang Mai University. One day two of them gave me a copy of an American journal which featured an article on school bullying. "What is 'bullying'?" they asked. "What does it refer to?"

I explained bullying and asked them the Thai word for 'bullying'. They remained mystified.

"There is no word. Why would anyone behave like that to a smaller, weaker person? Why would the stronger child not protect the weaker one, the little brother?"

Since then I've been observing playgrounds more closely whenever I visit schools. I have seen fighting and I have seen bigger boys casually swatting smaller ones to remind them of the pecking order. But no bullying. I've spoken to Thai teachers and playground supervisors and tell the same story. It's just not part of their culture.

Cooperation

We Westerners like to talk about entrepreneurialism. Thais *practice* it. There must be three self-employed Thais for every one American, Brit, or Aussie. And they know how to cooperate. They know that, for a society to survive over time, everyone needs to be a player in the game. "Win-lose" is not the Thai style.

Thais are strong supporters of Thai businesses, from the large to the microscopically small, making it difficult for foreign-owned companies to get a foothold. Imagine trying to compete against a business whose premises are the owner's carport, whose staff is the owner's mother (who lives upstairs and knows all of her customers and their kids by name) who marks up his merchandise by 15% instead of the customary 40%, and stays open until 10 o'clock on Sunday nights. *That's* tough competition!

And at the same time as they cooperate, Thais love independence. They are unenthusiastic employees but give them a chance and they'll make a business out of anything. They don't need a million dollars. They take whatever they've got right now and start.

My favorite example of cooperation is in the vast forecourt of the Chiang Mai mall shown here. Even though the owner invested hundreds of millions of dollars to build this air conditioned mall he doesn't object to what goes on right in front of his main door. Dozens of little food vendors set up right in front of his tenant, Sizzler's, million-dollar restaurant, blocking it entrance.

As the sun sets, arriving shoppers are forced to navigate hundreds of tables and racks arrayed on the steps and courtyard. You'd swear it was an obstacle course. Everything imaginable is for sale on those folding tables, from food and clothes to massages; most of it cheaper than the identical articles sold inside the mall.

For vendors who can't afford a folding table (you need a truck to transport a folding table), the solution is simple: a plastic table cloth laid in front of one of the folding tables.

That means that the plastic-table-cloth-merchants are blocking access to the folding-table-merchants who are blocking access to the mall-merchants who are paying high rent to attract the customers who are trying to get in!

But this is Thailand, so everyone just makes room for everyone else and life flows on good-naturedly.

That's the essence of Thailand's unique lifestyle. I come to this mall at least once a month just to marvel at it. And that's what I mean when I talk about a *culture* in this book: it's a pre-solved environment that takes everyone's needs into account.

Freedom
You will enjoy a degree of freedom here that disappeared from Western countries when our governments starting protecting us–first from ourselves and then from 'terrorism'. Thais have endured their share of real terrorism, but they haven't let it affect them. So police and security presence are light, as befits a free people.

However, with freedom comes responsibility. You are responsible not only for your own actions, but for others' heedlessness. That means that you must keep your wits about you: your eyes, ears, and nose. Watch where you walk, for example. Sidewalks are used for just about everything imaginable: parking; dumping building supplies; booths and stalls; signposts; tree stumps; the list is endless. In daylight this can be challenging; at night the difficulty doubles. It doesn't bother the Thais and after a few months here it won't bother you because your level of personal awareness will have risen. Until then, watch your step.

Everything You Know is Wrong

There's a temptation to imagine that, thanks to the Internet and globalization, everyone in the world is pretty much on the same page. That's certainly the impression that our media give us.

Nothing could be further from the truth. Westerners and Asians have very different mindsets and approach things from radically different perspectives. Since the failure to understand these differences often leads to misunderstanding, mistrust, and heartbreak, it's wise to learn about them sooner rather than later. So here is a summary of our assumptions:

One. Everyone has the same basic cognitive processes. Maori herders, !Kung hunter-gatherers, and dot-com entrepreneurs all rely on the same tools for perception, memory, causal analysis, categorization, and inference.

Two. When people in one culture differ from those in another in their beliefs, it can't be because they have different cognitive processes, but because they are exposed to different aspects of the world, or because they have been taught different things.

Three. "Higher order" processes of reasoning rest on the formal rules of logic: for example, a proposition can't be both true *and* false.

Four. Reasoning is separate from what is reasoned about. The same process can be used to think about utterly different things and a given thing can be reasoned about using any number of different procedures.

All wrong! Asians' attitudes, training, culture, and habits allow them to successfully break all these 'universal' rules. It turns out that there's nothing universal about them; they're just our Western cultural prejudices. To get a full understanding of this important difference, get *The Geography of Thought: How Asians and Westerners Think Differently...and Why*, by Richard E. Nisbett. If you're serious about moving East, it's a must-read.

East *Doesn't* Meet West

Since Asian cultures have lasted for thousands of years, and since they largely avoided the Great Financial Crisis we've begun to wonder if there might be something about their approach that's worth studying. When you get here you'll have ample opportunity to see how things are done. In the meantime, here are some clues gleaned from *The Geography of Thought*:

Medicine: Medicine in the West retains the analytic, object-oriented, and interventionist approaches that were common thousands of years ago: Find the offending part and remove or alter it. Medicine in the East is far more holistic and has never been in the least inclined towards surgery or other heroic interventions. Health is a result of a balance of favorable forces in the body; illness is due to a complex interaction of forces that must be met by equally complex, usually natural, mostly herbal remedies and preventives. (It's for this reason that our workshops include a very thorough consultation with one of Asia's leading practitioners of traditional medicine, who makes this point to her patients. It's a very personal, real-life introduction to the culture).

Law: The goal in Eastern conflict resolution is more likely to be hostility-reduction; compromise is assumed to be the likely result. Westerners call on universal principles of justice to push their goals and judges and juries feel obligated to make decisions that they believe to hold true for everyone in approximately the same circumstances.

Debate: Managers in Thailand tend to deal with conflict with other managers by simple avoidance of the situation, whereas Americans are far more likely to attempt persuasion. What is intrusive and dangerous in the East is considered a means for getting at the truth in the West. Westerners place and almost religious faith in the free marketplace of ideas. Bad ideas are no threat, at least over the long run, because they will be seen for what they are and can be discussed in public. There has never been such an assumption in the East and there is not today.

Contracts: To us, a deal is a deal. Contracts are sacred. In the East, agreements are treated as tentative guides for the future. Contracts should therefore be reviewed whenever either party's circumstances change. This makes for much better long-term relationship, even at the expense of short-term profits.

International Relations: To people in the East causation is never black and white or one-sided. Everything is interrelated, so they see things holistically. Rather than trying to see who is 'guilty' or 'wrong', they look to assign responsibility to both parties. Maybe not equally, but our phrase, "It takes two to tango" expresses their attitude.

Human Rights: Westerners think that individuals are separate, autonomous actors and they enter into contracts with one another and with the state that entails clear rights, freedoms, and duties. But East Asians see people as components of a culture, as parts of a much more important whole. So **individual rights** are quite minor when compared to **individual responsibilities** to society. It's an entirely different concept of rights and what an individual is.

Religion: The thousands of religious wars that we have experienced in the West are largely unknown in the East. Their holistic approach to life means that there is no room for exclusive 'right/wrong' dichotomies. It's both/and, yin/yang all the way. That's why you'll meet Thais who are meat-eating Buddhists who also practice Confucianism and Christianity. Whatever *your* notion of God is, it's OK with them.

Real-Life Examples: *Nam Jai*: น้ำใจ

Nam jai, 'generosity' and *sam-neuk boon koon,* 'repayment' or 'honoring debts' are concepts familiar to anyone, east or west. But there's more to both concepts in Thai culture, as I learned the hard way.

When I first moved to Thailand a Thai friend had shown me around and helped me get settled. Then, one day, much later, she burst out with what were obviously feelings of betrayal and abandonment. I hadn't been loyal to her or her family, and I hadn't been sufficiently respectful towards her lately.

I was staggered. After all, when I met her, she was struggling to launch a coffee shop in an unpromising location and things were not going well. Since 'marketing' is a foreign concept to Thais and one that is native to Australians, I understood her problem immediately and set up an online and on-street marketing program that worked well and got customers coming in the door. In my feelings, I had repaid my debt to her adequately. Why was she carrying on like this, long after the matter was closed?

I asked a fellow-expat that night if he could explain my friend's behavior. He went to his bookshelf and pulled down a recently published book, **Thailand Fever**, by Chris Pirazzi. If you're seriously considering moving here, buy it and read it. It's fascinating and fun and it will help you avoid the kind of pitfall I'd tumbled into. With Chris' help, I'll try to explain what had happened:

Nam Jai – น้ำใจ – Everything in Thailand starts with *nam-jai*, literally "heart-juice of the heart" or "heart-flow". We Westerners have been taught to value independence, but Thais judge themselves and others based on the degree to which they show *nam-jai*. *Nam-jai* is "generosity": giving your time, resources, and attention to others just for the good feeling it generates in both. Someone who demonstrates *nam-jai* won't ask for money or repayment in exchange for their generosity. Thais even feel uneasy accepting payment offered for their generosity because this suggests that she did it for the payment instead of the good will.

Thais don't travel much (expense and the difficulty in getting visas for 'developed' nations) so most Thais assume that you are like them and that you must derive your self-esteem from your demonstration of *nam-jai*.

For example, your Thai girlfriend is proud of you and wants to show you off as a generous person. Without asking you directly–she just assumes it–she'll give you opportunities to be generous. She may take you out to dinner with friends. She won't say "P' Godfree, do you mind paying for my friends' meals?" Instead, she'll assume that you, as a person who is older and has more money than her friends, will want to show your generosity by paying for all her friends. Westerners like me hate behavior like this. It's shameless manipulation. Does she think I'm her sugar daddy?

But, remember, it gives Thais self-esteem to be generous. Your girlfriend and her family are not trying to take advantage of you. They are doing the same thing they would do with a Thai man who they think might be able and willing to help the family.

In the usual case her family will be poorer than you. They'll never be able to repay anything close to the amount you've been giving to them and their friends. But...they will *always* remember your generosity. Since this incident I've spoken to many Westerners who struggled for months or years over their feelings of being exploited. Then, suddenly, when circumstances changed, they were surprised to find themselves at the receiving end of *nam-jai*. All because of *sam-neuk-boon-koon*.

Real-Life Examples: *Sam-neuk-boon-koon* – สำนึกบุญคุณ

Cultures based on *nam-jai* survive and thrive because of the *boon-koon* system, specifically the value of *sam-neuk-boon-koon*. *Sam-neuk-boon-koon* is the balance that makes the system work. Thais are raised from childhood to Sam-neuk-boon-koon: to repay favors that people do for you (honor your debts).

But there's much more to it than that. Suppose Nun, a manager at Thirabongse Company, does a favor for his old friend Nid by finding him a job at the company. Nid was raised to *sam-neuk-boon-koon* and so he:

One: commits to being available to repay Nun's favor whenever Nun needs something.
Two: demonstrates his appreciation of Nun's generosity by showing Nun respect, deference, and consideration in his behavior and speech.
Three: frequently reminds himself of Nun's generous act and his own commitment to return Nun's favor.

Thai society is a cycle of *nam-jai* and s*am-neuk-boon-koon*. People do favors out of *nam-jai* and don't ask for anything in return. Those who receive favors *sam-neuk-boon-koon* and voluntarily make themselves available to help the giver in return.

Everyone serving and everyone being served. It's a cycle of mutual obligation that creates a remarkably stable, harmonious society.

But this is Thailand, and that's not the end of the story. Suppose Nid spends a couple of weekends doing (unpaid) overtime at Thirabongse Company to help out Nun. Surely that clears their accounts: it's more time and effort than his friend exerted to get the job for him after all?

Not at all. Suppose further that Nun needs Nid to come in *every* weekend for a couple of months to help him out? If Nin were a Westerner he'd feel annoyed and exploited. But Nid is Thai, so he *rushes* to come in early every weekend until the job is done. Why? Because–finally!–he has an opportunity to demonstrate *nam jai* to his friend Nun.

And so the circle of obligation and service is maintained and strengthened. Multiply that almost-invisible example by 65 million people over their entire lifetimes and you can understand why Thai culture is so cohesive.

Fitting In

This may sound silly but you'll find that it's very effective: Act silly! Thais are reserved and shy when dealing with *farangs*. They don't travel much and they don't know much about our culture, so they tend to act a little stiff around us. You can break the ice in a way that works every time: by acting a little silly.

Thais love to laugh and they have a very simple sense of humor. I've found that almost every circumstance can be improved by simply pulling a silly face or making an exaggerated gesture, pretending to cry (while smiling, of course) or some such nonsensical reaction.

Try it yourself. You'll be met with peals of laughter and a sudden warming of the situation. A *farang*? Acting *silly*? Nothing funnier, I assure you.

Once a Thai lady in my *moo baan* pointed out that I was wearing my T-shirt inside-out. I made desperate, exaggerated attempts to cover my shame, flailing my arms and trying to cover the evidence of my mistake. As I walked away she and fellow-residents were supporting each other as tears of laughter rolled down their faces.

If you're shy about acting silly, then practice your smiling. Smiling in unexpected or tense situations is almost as effective. Honestly, Thais will do almost anything to avoid or defuse an awkward situation and, if you take the initiative, they'll follow enthusiastically.

Have a question about this chapter? A suggestion?
Email me: godfree@thailandretirementhelpers.com
I'll get back to you within 48 hours.

GOOD MANNERS

Thailand is a culture of respect and, like most oriental cultures, Thai culture is formal and non-confrontational. *Everyone* strives to conform to the cultural norms. After thousands of years of experimentation they have concluded that there are better ways of resolving problems than through confrontation. So relax, chill, smile, bow, apologize and–surprise!–90% of problems resolve themselves.

We've already seen that Thais are *both* more formal *and* friendlier than we are when they greet each other with the w*ai*, a blessing, and a smile. This alone gets you through 99% of social situations. Here are a few more do's and don'ts that will distinguish you as a polite, cultivated *farang*.

The Royal Family–Video

Thais' attitude to hierarchy is different from ours. Their approach to their Royal Family, for example, carries down through the entire social structure, just as it does in Japan.

The Royal Family and the King in particular, are greatly respected by Thais. There is an entire TV channel devoted to them, and their likenesses appear everywhere. Thousands of formal, framed photographs of them are sold every day in Thailand. Speaking disrespectfully of the King is illegal here, under a law known in the West as *lese majeste*. With rare exceptions it is applied only to Thais who deliberately and publicly seek to provoke a reaction. **Here's a video that will give you an idea of how Thais regard their royal family.**

To give you a feeling for how people generally feel, a Thai friend once found me stretched out on the couch where I was lying on some money that had slipped out of my pocket. She scolded me and made me stand while she removed the coins and notes because, she said, "That's the King's picture you're lying on."

Similarly, standing over someone older, wiser, or more enlightened than yourself is also considered disrespectful since it implies social superiority. As a sign of courtesy, it is considered polite to lower your head as you pass a group of people. Aggressive stances such as crossed arms or waving your arms are considered boorish and uncultivated. When in doubt, watch the Thais.

This may all sound a bit much to newcomers but you will be surprised by how quickly it becomes second nature. After all, you'll have 65 million Thais' example to follow.

Table Manners

At table, people eat their meals with a spoon. Even in those rare cases when they have steak, they will often cut it up first then put it to their mouths with a spoon. Though a fork is served with the meal, it is only used to push food onto your spoon, and never put to your mouth.

When eating, it is considered very rude to blow your nose or to lick your fingers. Use your right hand to pick up food eaten with the fingers. The left hand is considered unclean and should not be used to eat, receive gifts, or shake hands.

After the meal, Thais often pick their teeth but they cover their mouths with their left hand while doing so. Of course, if you are eating alone or with other *farangs*, these rules can be set aside.

Dress and Clothing

It is both common sense and good manners to dress conservatively when dealing with border officials, customs clerks, local police, and bureaucrats. Visitors who forget this can cause unnecessary ill feeling.

It's generally best to dress conservatively, as the Thais do. Unless you're at the beach, don't wear skimpy shorts, halter tops, low-cut blouses, or anything else that will offend the locals. Slacks and shirt are recommended for men in urban environments. Women should keep well covered. Swim-wear is only acceptable on the beach.

Touching: Personal and Bodily Space

Western society is rather touchy-feely. In the East such familiarity is not practiced in public. Try to avoid touching Thais; it is too intimate a gesture and an invasion of personal space. If you do, don't worry. They've seen lots of Western movies and they understand that we barbarians mean no harm.

Along with most Eastern peoples, Thais regard the head to be the most sacred part of the body. The *kwan*, the spiritual force of life, resides there. So don't pat a Thai on the head even in the friendliest of circumstances.

The feet are the least sacred, so when sitting they should not point at anyone. That's why most Thais sit on the floor with their feet tucked under them, or cross-legged. To point, particularly with foot, is insulting. The worst insult to a Thai is to point your unholy foot at his sacred head. Keep your feet under control; fold them underneath when sitting down, don't point them toward another person, and *never* place your feet on a table.

Expressing Emotions

Thais say that patience, humor, and *jai yen* (a cool heart) bring results. The word 'heart', *jai*, is common in Thai. Here are some phrases you will hear frequently:

Jai yen–cool heart. The idea is that you remain cool, calm and collected at all times. The Thais often use this phrase to remind someone who gets hot and bothered. If you ever show impatience or strong emotions you will not impress the locals. And men should *never* lose their temper with a woman. It is very bad form. (The reverse does *not* apply!)

Jai dee–good heart. Kindness, especially to people who have less than you, or the doing of good deeds, is looked upon fondly in Thailand and is often referred to in Buddhist terms as 'gaining merit'.

Jai ron–hot heart. It is often used to describe people who are hot tempered or impatient, particularly *farangs*. It is not quite an insult, but if someone describes you as *jai ron*, you need to chill.

Greng jai–considerate, thoughtful. A person shows *greng jai* when, instead of burdening their boss (or anyone else) with a problem, they first try to discover a solution, and then approach him.

Mai pen rai–no problem, never mind, it doesn't matter. Thais use it liberally, and if you want to survive in Thailand you'll want to use it often too, if only to maintain sanity. If you complain to a vendor, for example, about a shortcoming in something you just purchased, he's likely to tell you "*mai pen rai*" and go on his way having satisfied himself that all is now well!

While we're on the subject of defective merchandise: returns are practically unknown in Thailand. You buy it, you own it.

The exception is Western-owned hypermarkets, which allow returns. As I tell the story elsewhere in this book, my Thai friend was initially mortified with embarrassment when I insisted we return a defective appliance to the (French-owned) hypermarket. Days later she was still telling her friends about how her money was returned immediately, without argument. *Farangs* are strange!

It's wise to study Thais' emotional intelligence because Westerners often think that Oriental people are unemotional. Far from it. Thais are sensitive to, and considerate of, emotions. They just express them differently.

Have a question about this chapter? A suggestion?
Email me: godfree@thailandretirementhelpers.com
I'll get back to you within 48 hours.

MONEY: DOUBLING YOUR INCOME

I spent my first year in Thailand living on $1240/month. Because the cost of living here is so low, that gave me a $3,000/mo. standard of living–more than doubling my purchasing power, as you'll see from some of the examples below.

I lived a stone's throw from the leafy campus of Chiang Mai University in air-conditioned Sa-Nguan Malee Mansion (the building you see above) ate out three times a day, rented a moped, and lived a comfortable, leisurely life. Had I been with a partner with a similar income we could have lived almost luxuriously.

To help you understand how that's possible, remember this benchmark: a beginning engineer here makes $500/month after graduation from university.

When you live in Thailand you have one of life's great luxuries: forgetting about money and focusing on living. That's the real point of this book.

For Americans: Social Security Abroad

Australians cannot receive government pensions while living abroad and Brits are penalized. The US Social Security Administration places no restrictions on where American citizens live. But if you move abroad you do have to inform SSA, tell them where to deposit your check, and keep them updated.

Many people don't know that U.S. citizens can receive Social Security payments outside the United States. Visit this page to check your eligibility and learn how to keep it while you're living in Thailand: **Social Security Payments Outside the United States** .

Just for Fun–Video

Before we get serious about money, **here's an amusing video** of how a young Brit, Alex Putnam of the adventure organizers, **Open Chiang Mai**, got by on 100 Baht/day. That's $3.30/day, or $100/month. It's not a sustainable lifestyle tor one hat will appeal to retirees but it's a glimpse into backpacker life – for the young. Forget about a balanced diet!

Two Social Security Budgets for Thailand

Realistic expectations and a sound budget are the key to carefree living when your *only* support is your Social Security check. Even though I lived well on mine for my first 12 momnths I turned to a genuine expert on detailed budgeting, Nancy Lindley. Nancy has many years of bookkeeping experience who not only makes personal budgets but also keeps to them *and* keeps careful note of unexpected.

Another reason I asked Nancy for these budgets is that she has a second calling. She cares for expatriates here when they fall on hard times and have no-one else to turn to. She visits them in hospital, contacts relatives, talks to the consulate, and spends countless hours repatriating people who cannot afford to pay for care and must return to the US, the UK, or Australia for serious medical conditions. So she has seen a dimension of expatriate life that few of us have even thought about.

I asked Nancy to draw up two budgets, one for half the average Social Security check and one for twice the average, and to comment on each. I've added my comments after hers. Both budgets are for Chiang Mai. For Bangkok add 15%, for the countryside subtract 15%. Please contact me with budget questions. These are current as of 2013.

$600/month Social Security Budget

CATEGORY	THAI BAHT ($1=30)	COMMENTS
RENT	5,000	Long-term rents start at $2,000
UTILITIES	1,000	Electric, TV, Water
INTERNET	600	1 hr/day @ Internet cafe
TRANSPORT	600	30 Songthaew rides/mo.
FOOD	6,000	Careful selection for nutrition
PERSONAL CARE	300	Toiletries, hair cuts, etc.
ENTERTAINMENT	1,000	Nice meal, movie, day trip
MISCELLANEOUS	500	Visa maintenance, phone time, laundry
TOTAL	**15,000**	

Nancy's Comments

I've seen single people lead nice, pleasant lives on this budget. Here's how they do it:

- They have a fan (no a/c) room on the lower (cooler) floor of a guesthouse in the old city,
- They walk just about everywhere,
- Use the AUA library for books,
- Eat breakfast at the UN Irish Pub where they watch American sports (shown live in the mornings),
- Take lessons at a wat (temple), etc.
- There is no room in this budget for a steady girlfriend or regular beer-drinking habit.

- Also, **it's imperative to have savings to cover medical costs -- which are not reflected in this budget. Or perhaps health insurance -- again, not covered in this budget.**

I've known several guys who have a pension of 30,000 - 40,000 baht/month, yet they live on a 15,000 baht budget and save the rest for medical emergencies and to build a bank account to justify a retirement visa. This takes discipline, which disappears once someone acquires a Thai girlfriend who learns about the existence of a savings account!

Now here's the budget for a couple with a combined monthly income of about $2500/month -- the average SS payment for a couple.

$2500/month Social Security Budget

RENT	14,000	A new, 2-br condo
UTILITIES	3,000	Incl. a/c
INTERNET	1200	Cable Internet
LAUNDRY, MAID	2500	Weekly maid
TRANSPORT	2400	Songthaews/ scooter rent
FOOD, DINING	25,000	Some wine or beer
PERSONAL CARE	4,000	Manicure, massage/ mo.
ENTERTAINMENT	6,000	Nice weekly meals
INSURANCE,	9,500	incl. out-of-pocket

MEDICAL		medcal
VISA MAINTENANCE	800	
PHONE TIME	500	
MAJOR TRAVEL	6,100	or big-ticket purchases
TOTAL	75,000	

Nancy's Comments on the Deluxe Budget

There is much more room to play with this budget. I assume:
- The couple is renting a condo in town. Housing rentals are cheaper in outlying areas, but transportation costs are higher -- with a car a necessity.
- No sane retiree is going to rely solely on a motorscooter [see my note, below, on this]
- The couple is fairly healthy,
- Don't have to eat expensive imported food for every meal,
- Drinks wine/beer very moderately

My Observations

As I mentioned, I lived on $1240/mo. during my first year in Thailand. I made lots of mistakes and wasted lots of money but, after 6 months, found I could live quite comfortably. For example,
- I found a long-term studio rental in town for 2,000 Baht ($70) /month. [see photo] Utilities added $10.
- My long-term scooter rental for 3,000 Baht/month provides regular servicing, new tires as needed, and a new scooter every 12 months. I've had no scooter problems.

- I stay within Nancy's recommended food budget of 6,000 Baht and have never eaten a healthier, more delicious diet in my life.
- I'm 73 and not eligible for medical insurance so I pay 500 Baht/mo. for accident insurance.
- That means all my regular medical expenses are out-of-pocket. Thai health care is excellent and cheap. I just paid 18,000 Baht ($600) for a root canal and crown, for example.
- Toiletries are cheap. An organic skin cream costs 60 Baht; a haircut 60 Baht.
- 'Entertainment' is what you make of it. I like wandering around observing how the Thai culture works.
- The Internet provides plenty of information and entertainment, and I go to the pub to watch major sporting events since I don't like having TV at home. The pub doesn't care if I don't order anything. Thailand is a civilized society.
- Cellphones are very cheap; overseas calls are expensive. Skype or have friends call you.
- Nancy is not kidding about Thai girls and savings accounts. They are not mercenary; it's just part of Thai culture. You are a rich *farang* whether you think so or not.
- There are decent restaurants where you can have three bottles of ice-cold beer served at your table for 160 Baht. Split them with a friend and you're in good shape.

Your 'Free' Trip to Thailand

With flexibility and some strategizing you can pay for your trip to Thailand by saving on inevitable expenses. A lot of workshop attendees do this and enjoy essentially free trips.

I know because we organize their appointments at hospitals, dentists, and surgeons. They sign up for long-delayed surgeries and dental work and save enough to cover the entire cost of the workshop and travel. Most surgical procedures, for example, cost less here than the deductible in the USA.

Before you even get here the first step is to reduce your airfare. Bangkok is one of the most popular destinations on earth with the world's most competitive fares, especially for last-minute purchases.

And Kuala Lumpur, Malaysia, is the Asian hub for discount fares. So start by checking flights through Kuala Lumpur International Airport (KL). Most cheap Asian fares originate and terminate in KL.

Reality break: KL is cheap because the terminal is cheap. You'll probably have to walk from your plane to the terminal, and that can be quite a hike in the tropical heat, lugging carryon. The terminal is not air conditioned, and getting around it can be a puzzle, since signage is confusing. So here in the East, as in the West, there are no free lunches.

An excellent airfares tool for Americans is **SkyAuction**. Spend a few minutes studying the bidding process, then start low ball bidding. Fun *and* profitable, as airlines rush to fill their last few seats at almost any price. **Kayak** is another good site for finding conventional discount fares.

Brits and Aussies can also go to **Adioso**. It covers all airlines, including Air Asia, which combines budget fares with premium service. Adioso lets you set your route and price, and then alerts you as soon as there's a match. I've seen fares that are freakishly low, but some typical recent bargains include Thailand return fares from LAX: $862; London: £465; Sydney: $797. That's the cost of a ticket to an entirely new life.

Clothes

Stop buying clothes now. You can have clothes tailored to any pattern, especially out of silk, or buy them off the rack at a fraction of the cost at home. This is particularly important to Australians whose clothing prices are many times Thai prices.

Accommodation

You can stay inexpensively in Thailand. There are ultra-cheap places, like rooms for $60/month. Let me know if you need help, as conditions change depending on the season.

Food

I try to eat something new every evening. My average meal costs $4 and I rarely spend
More than $10--and that's when I order two large bottles of premium beer with a three-course meal.

25 Ways to Save Money in Thailand

1. **Come in the Summer:** Thailand is much cheaper between May and November. Rooms, food and vehicle rental often discounted. There are far fewer tourists around, and you're more likely to receive personal service.

2. **Stay on the Mainland**: Remember how expensive Hawaii is? That's because everything you buy on an island is transported by boat or plane. Island life is always more expensive than living on the mainland.

3. **Choose Basic Accommodation**: Simple rooms cost less than 150 baht ($5) a night or you can share with another bargain hunter to split costs. Dorm rooms are even cheaper.

4. **Travel at Night, by Train, or by Bus**: Plane fare from BKK to Chiang Mai is $70 each way and you see nothing. You can go a long way for a few baht on overnight trains because you won't need a room that night. An air-conditioned seat or a sleeping compartment is around $25 each way BKK to Chiang Mai, about 1,000 km. Third-class rail is even cheaper. Air-conditioned day bus rides show you the whole country for less than half that and you kill two birds with one stone.

5. **Use Local Transport:** Local buses and, *songthaews* (shared taxi/pickups) go everywhere in town for around 20 Baht (70¢).

6. **Hitch Hike**: Riskier, as it is everywhere, but many people hitchhike around Thailand. Do offer money for gas, even though it's rarely accepted.

7. **Avoid Western Food:** Foreign food is mostly imported and not well prepared. For the price of a single pizza you can eat three Thai meals a day for three days.

8. **Eat Like the Locals**: Thais love food, and you will always be close to a market selling curry and rice ($2) or a small restaurant making Thai food to order. Just watch the locals and point to whatever looks good, smile, and say "khap". Roadside stalls are literally everywhere, especially at night, and meals cost around $2.

9. **Don't Tip**: Thais don't tip. You need not.

10. **Accept Offers of Food, Drink and Accommodation**: Thais are friendly and gracious and if you're around them you'll be invited for a drink or a meal. The offer of a bed for the night is a generous gesture, but consider it carefully.

11. **Water is Good for You:** In this flood-prone country it's best to drink bottled water. Buy big bottles in local grocery stores rather than small bottles in restaurants or convenience stores; drink plenty of free water whenever you eat a meal. You can even fill your water bottle free in banks, hotel foyers, and Buddhist temples. There are RO (reverse osmosis) dispensers on every street corner that dispense 2 gallons for 3 Bt. (10¢).

12. **Alcohol is a Luxury:** Supermarket beer is $1.65 for a large, cold bottle. Outside Bangkok you can have it served at your table for $2.10. Lao Kao, the cheapest alcoholic drink, is a harsh local spirit that's palatable mixed with Coca-Cola. Thai whisky, like 100 Pipers, is cheap and surprisingly drinkable.

13. **Use Free Entertainment**: Thais exercise at local parks; often there are free aerobics groups, basketball, tennis, tagraw (an amazing mix of football, volleyball, and kung fu), tai chi, or concerts and festivals. You can watch free films at resorts or read a free newspaper in a library or a hotel. As a rich *farang* you can waltz into the most luxurious hotel lobbies and take advantage of the A/C, the latest newspapers, even free cups of tea.

14. **Buy Clothes and Personal Items in Thailand**: Clothes are very cheap and well suited to the hot climate. I buy a new cotton long-sleeved drawstring pants and great long-sleeved shirts for $14 total. Toiletries are much cheaper than back home, with free soap in some rooms and sometimes in shared bathrooms.

15. **Bring Your Own Specialized Equipment:** For special activities like diving, it's often better to bring your own gear rather than renting it. Most such stuff here made in China and not the same quality you're used to.

16. **Watch Your Money:** Thailand is a cash economy which makes budgeting easy. Put your daily budget, in cash, in your pocket each morning and let that be your guide. This saves you being distracted by obsessive budgeting on the one hand and tempted by credit cards on the other.

17. **Minimize Money Charges**: You'll be charged $5 for withdrawing money from an ATM plus your own bank's exchange rate plus any other charges they can get away with. So bring cash with you and, if you need to make an ATM withdrawal, take out your daily maximum: usually around $500.

18. **Do You Really Need a Guide Book?** Do your research on the Internet before you leave. Store the relevant information on your Smartphone or a USB memory stick and use an Internet cafe here. Pick up free brochures when you get here. Or just buy a guide book at a local used book store.

19. **Haggle**: Bargaining for some items is expected in Thailand. Anything from a market is fair game, but keep it real when trying to

get an extra few baht discount. Room prices can be negotiated, especially in low season and for longer stays.

20. Do Your Own Laundry: A 10 Baht packet of washing powder and a few minutes each day is all that you need. If you buy loose, light clothing here, it will dry in minutes in the hot sun. Buy a sarong here to use instead of a heavy towel. Washing machines are everywhere (in the street!) and a 5 lb. (2 kg.) load is 66c. There's also a laundry on every block that will happily do your laundry for $2.

21. **Know the Rules of the Road**: They're like the ones at home, though Thais drive on the left. Bring an international driving license with you (get it from your local motoring club) and *always* carry it when driving. Always wear seat belts in cars and helmets on motorbikes, or you risk a fine. They're only $7-10, but a big nuisance. If you are booked for a traffic infraction you will be required to surrender your license until you've paid your fine.

22. **Obey the Local Laws**: Littering is an offense in Thailand, and people have been fined for dropping cigarette butts on the ground. Police will pay more attention to the actions of a foreigner, so be aware, especially in Bangkok.

23. **Don't Be a Victim**: Google "Thailand scams" and study up. There's nothing original, but it's best to know in advance that you're not in Kansas anymore. For example, at the airport, ask the fare *in advance*. Avoid tuk-tuks. Read the safety tips in the appendix to this book.

24. **Get Paid to Travel**: Again, Google this idea. Talk to your local newspaper, etc., or act as a buyer for someone or a business at home if you have expertise. Enliven your blog (see the Ten Best Blogs in this book for inspiration). Our workshops include a seminar devoted just to this.

25. **Avoid Tourist Traps:** It sounds obvious, but there are several places, like Pattaya, Phuket and Ko Samui that are overpriced and overcrowded. You'll have more fun off the beaten track visiting

remote temples and national parks. And if you want to spend some beach time, try Nakhon Si Thammarat where the unique food is a big plus.

Have a question about this chapter? A suggestion?
Email me **godfree@thailandretirementhelpers.com**.
I'll get back to you in 48 hours

REAL LIFE IN THAILAND
Another letter home

A neighborhood Thai family has taught me about the life of working-class Thais. They – grandmother, son, daughter, and two kids aged 4 and 7 – live in a crowded basement room so dim, poor and mean that they have never allowed me to see it. When I arrive they come rushing out and we sit in the driveway (shared with several other families in the little backstreet apartment complex, or *moo baan*) and eat our evening meal.

My US Social Security income is $1,200/month, which seems laughable because, before the Crash, it was $10,000. But to my Thai family it is an impressive amount. Twice what an engineer earns.

Each month the family insists on looking at my online bank statement in wonderment: money for nothing. Appearing magically in my bank account every month without my lifting a finger to earn it. I even know in advance when it will arrive! For them the arrival of money is always uncertain.

They don't have a bank account. Their tiny incomes are spent immediately, on survival, so there's no time for the money to linger in a bank.

Their indispensable cell phones must be refilled in 60¢ increments so that everyone can coordinate picking up children after school and who's working what shifts. It's a day-to-day existence, and if the shared motor scooter gets a flat tire it's an emergency for everyone, even though the repair only costs 200Bt. ($7). Sometimes, if money is tight, the scooter must be left at the kids' school in lieu of late payment for school fees. Schooling is compulsory but not free.

When my money does appear all 6 of us get on our two scooters and head to the local Carrefour hypermarket, Big C. It's a huge treat because the ceilings are so high and the whole place is so spacious compared to their tiny rooms at home.

They love to wander around, just feeling the generosity of the place: you can twirl around without hitting a wall or another person! The kids can run and not hit anything! And in the summer the air-conditioning is like heaven! The lights are so bright! (They live with 9-watt compact fluorescent lighting at home to save energy).

The kids play in the market's all-plastic playground. There are no playgrounds in Thailand, so this is a grand treat.
Then we go to the food court where they order Western food like pizzas. Like most Asians they are lactose-intolerant but won't listen to my scolding about the kids' runny noses. And the biggest treat of all: Subway sandwiches.

These foods are considered evidence of Western progress and the height of sophistication. They linger over the meals and discuss them in minute detail.

It's winter here, and last week I noticed that they all had soft coughs. When I pressed them they said that it might be because they have to take outdoor cold showers since they have neither indoor toilets nor showers. So this week we spent an hour in the market's hardware section examining in great detail the on-demand water heaters and finally settled on a Panasonic model. I paid for it ($100) but, because my Thai language skills are still rudimentary, I understood little of what was going on. There was something in the negotiations with the sales clerk that they found astonishing.

Later I later asked them what it was. They struggled to find the word, since it was one that barely exists in Thai: the heater had a guarantee. The notion that they could return it if it malfunctioned was completely novel to them--and empowering.

Last night they all came over to my house glowing pink, scrubbed and radiant: they had just taken their first hot showers.

Friends—Video

Along with 30,000 other expats I live in Chiang Mai, the cultural capital of Thailand. As you would expect, retirees here are adventurous and pretty gregarious. Between us I've counted 32 activity groups, from cycling and photography to fish farming and organic gardening. So you needn't worry about how to fill your time.

There are more formal expat groups, too, and we meet twice monthly with the ambassadors and consuls from our national diplomatic corps, and with visiting and resident experts on every imaginable aspect of Thai life, law, and culture. They're an easygoing bunch and maintain a nice balance between having fun and doing real community service.

I've been in a few jams of my own creation since I settled here and have been astonished at how rapidly my new expat friends responded with offers of money, intervention, and the free use of their offices and staffs. It really restores your faith in human nature.

I've concluded that the reason we become cynical about our fellow humans is that at home our friends and neighbors don't get much chance to help one another: everything's handled. Out here we're a minority and pretty much on our own. So everyone pitches in. My new friends are one of the high points of my life here and that I don't want to relinquish. We go to great lengths in our workshops to introduce you to local expats whose experience is invaluable and whose occasional help is indispensable. And speaking of friends, **here's a video of my retiree friends discussing their expat lifestyle in Chiang Mai.**

Accommodation: Buying Vs. Renting

Traditionally, Thai homes were constructed of wood. Teak and rosewood were favorites in the old days. These beautifully-decorated homes can still be found. In fact, a friend of mine lives in one, with lawn, garage, 3 bedrooms and servant's quarters. His rent? 10,000 Baht ($340).

Modern condos like mine are sturdily constructed of reinforced concrete and tile. They are unlike our Western homes in interesting ways but they get the important things right: they're cool, airy, and clean.

Like many countries Thailand only permits Thais to own land. There are three ways to address this: Marry a Thai and buy in their name, become a Thai citizen, or buy a condo. Condos are exempt from the land-ownership rule and new ones start at $50,000.

I recommend waiting at least a year before buying property in Thailand. Renting is cheap and gives you time to investigate neighborhoods thoroughly. My 'real' home is a condo in the *moo baan* below. It's new, air-conditioned, with a 24-hour gate man and is on a quiet hillside street near the university.

Townhouses with a Difference: Moo Baans

A *moo baan* is a cross between a townhouse and a gated community, complete with security guards and a range of facilities. Many people, both Western and Thai, prefer them so let's take a look at the *moo baan*.

Most *moo baans* built recently, with Western-style amenities, offer a mix of apartments and small- or medium-sized townhouses or detached houses with one, two, or three bedrooms.

You'll have a choice of old-fashioned, Thai-style cement townhouses that often have dark interiors and only the basic facilities (Thai-style bathrooms and not western-style, for example) or, if it's a modern *moo baan*, contemporary housing with all the mod cons.

I recommend renting a free-standing house and not a townhouse, since connecting walls can be insufficient barriers to Thai neighbors who love playing karaoke at 2 a.m. In a detached house you have a better chance of getting a good night's sleep. Of course, if you're a party person Thailand's your paradise.

We Westerners like to complain that we've become isolated from one another and that individualism has gone too far. Thailand is the antidote to that complaint. Thais are very friendly and much more inquisitive than we are, so your Thai neighbors in a *moo baan* will be *much* more involved in your life than were your neighbors back home. They'll always want to know where you've been or where you're going. They'll ask you where you went last night and you'll say, 'To a restaurant'. That's not enough information for your neighbor: 'Alone, or with a friend?' will be the response. They'll gossip about you if you do something that's not 'normal' in Thailand (pretty much everything) and they'll cheerfully 'borrow', use, and abuse your property as they would their own.

The good news is that they're also the most hospitable (I get *daily* invitations for drinks or meals, or just to hang out. I'm not a very social person, so I'm constantly inventing excuses. It's a nice problem to have) people on earth. They're also kind, helpful neighbors: happy to keep an eye on your house while you're away and, if you ever have an accident, anxious to help.

Since accidents are rare and borrowing things (and forgetting to return them) is common, you might start to develop a negative attitude towards your Thai neighbors. Then something goes wrong in your life and you realize that you were just being a grump. Your *moo baan* neighbors will swing into action: take you to the hospital, translate for you, fend off the cops, bring you food, and watch over you like a protective mother. So chill out and enjoy your new culture.

Noise: Less expensive *moo baans* attract people with lower incomes who tend to be more tolerant of noise and much noisier when they party, which is often. Every night in fact. While it is not difficult to get them to tone it down (the security guard will ask them for you) it is probably better to choose more carefully and pay a little more.

Security: *Moo baans* usually have a neatly-uniformed security guard manning the gate. This is comforting when you're new to a country. The guards usually walk the entire property every 10-20 minutes so you can safely leave your doors and windows open, which cuts down on a/c bills. Of course, when you go out, lock up just as you would at home.

Facilities: There is hardly any inhabited area in Thailand that does not have a restaurant, especially since there are no zoning laws here. And if you don't like their food, the security guard will arrange free meal delivery. Believe it or not, McDonalds delivers here. Many *moo baans* have elaborate food facilities, including coffee shops and bakeries, and sometimes gyms, so check around before you commit.

Cost: The variation in accommodation costs is much wider than we are accustomed to. I have friends in *moo baans* who pay 2,100 Bt. ($70) a month for a studio apartment and others who shell out 65,000 Bt ($2,200) for a 3+ bedroom luxury pad with a pool, gym, and all mod cons. Houses have an equally wide range of rents. Since most *moo baans* have 6-month leases, you can usually bargain for quite substantial discounts – up to 30% – in exchange for a longer lease or cash up front.

Have a question about this chapter? A suggestion?
Email me: **godfree@thailandretirementhelpers.com**.
I'll get back to you within 48 hours.

MEDICAL AND DENTAL CARE

Health care in Thailand is not only superb, it's also cheap. So cheap that millions of visitors take vacations in Thailand and pay for them by having medical or dental work done. It's called 'medical tourism'.

I've used the Thai medical system and each time have come away impressed. The first time, a visit to the emergency ward, was so nice that I almost enjoyed it. Three doctors and many charming nurses fussed over me (glasses of water, heated blankets while I lay on the gurney) for hours making sure that I was OK. The bill: 500 Baht ($17).

The next visit was to an outpatient ward with a Thai friend's 7-year-old son. I had researched his symptoms on the Internet and diagnosed his illness and was eager to see how the doctors performed. They nailed it. They treated the boy on the spot and offered his mother the option of leaving him for overnight observation at no additional charge. She elected to take him home and I paid the bill on our way out: 200 Baht ($7).

My most recent experience involved a painful nerve condition called m*eralgia paresthetica*. I was confident that I had diagnosed it correctly so decided to treat myself. Imagine my delight when I found that Thai pharmacies *don't require prescriptions!* It was a self-medicator's dream.

I ordered and tried every drug that I read about online. My painkillers, 12 x 300 mg Neurontin, which cost $24 in the USA, are $7 here. And being able to bypass appointment-making, travel, and paying the doctor – just to get a prescription – was great.

Americans have difficulty believing good news about health because of the state of health care in the US. But Australians, New Zealanders and Brits, coming from countries which have much better health plans, are easier to convince.

Medical Costs

Performed in a US-certified Thai hospital by UK/US-certified physicians, almost any procedure pays for your trip. Here are some current Thai prices:

PROCEDURE	U.S. $	Thai Baht
Upper & Lower Blephalophasty	885	26,500
Liposuction	1,644	50,000
Hernia Surgery/Repair	1,776	50,200
Breast Augmentation	2,598	80,000
Full Face Lift Surgery	3,223	100,000
Tummy Tuck	3,584	110,000
Knee Joint Replacement	7,092	21,0000
Hip Joint Replacement	10,000	30,0000

Coronary Angioplasty	13,000	40,000
Gastric Bypass	13,000	40,000
Coronary Angioplasty	13,000	40,000

There are more detailed comparisons–between world-famous private Thai hospitals and Thai Government hospitals in my book, **Medical Insurance in Thailand**.

We've found that it's not enough to just *tell* people about Thai medical care, you actually have to experience it. So our workshops provide a full general physical at the University Medical Center, for everyone who requests it, at no charge. The same physical costs about $1200 in the USA. That way, they're ready to apply for medical insurance *and* their electronic medical record is already on file for immediate access anywhere in Thailand.

Hospital Charges
In Chiang Mai the typical private hospital room rate–including nurse and room service and meals–is $100-$200/day. Public hospitals are considerably cheaper.

Medical Insurance
This is an individual, complex matter because of the range of ages and options: from basic outpatient coverage at a Thai Government hospital all the way to full international, deluxe coverage with medical evacuation options. Because it's such a concern for expats living in Thailand, and because it's complex, I've written a 60 page report, **Medical Insurance in Thailand**. Here's the table of contents:
    1. NO INSURANCE
    2. SELF- INSURANCE
    3. GET HEALTHY

4. GO MINIMAL
5. GET A JOB AND GET LIFETIME GOVERNMENT INSURANCE
6. NORMAL HEALTH INSURANCE
7. TRAVEL INSURANCE
8. THAI INSURANCE COMPANIES
9. HOSPITALS IN THAILAND
10. THE HOSPITAL HIERARCHY
11. REAL HOSPITAL COSTS
12. APPLYING FOR INSURANCE
13. INSURANCE COMPANY CONTACTS
14. THAILAND'S HOSPITALS: CERTIFICATIONS
15. IF YOU HAVE A ROAD ACCIDENT
16. QUESTIONS FOR YOUR BROKER
17. HEALTH FACTORS

When you're getting serious about moving to Thailand, you can **download it at Amazon.com.**

Doctors and Nurses–Video

I asked my friends to talk about their experiences with Thai doctors and nurses. **Here's the video of what they had to say.**

Dental Fees–Video

There's good news about dentistry in Thailand. Many Thai dentists, like Thai doctors, are trained in Germany, Australia, the UK, or the USA. They speak excellent English, take their time with you, their equipment and procedures are futuristic, and their work is excellent. Fillings with space-age materials cost me $32. Getting your teeth fixed is the quickest way to pay for your airfare. The savings on many procedures can easily pay for your entire trip. Some current Thailand dentistry prices:

PROCEDURE	US $	Thai Baht
Oral Exam, Consultation	16	500

OPG X-Ray (Digital)	32	100
Air-Flow Cleaning	52	155
Filling, Composite Resin	26-103	800-3,000
Inlay, Onlay Ceramic	195-261	6,000-7,800
Laser Whitening	232	7,000
IPS Empress II Veneer	291	9,000
Ceramic Semi Precious Crown	452	13,000
Full Denture High Impact (1 Jaw)	565	16,500
Straumann SL Active Implant	2,421	73,000
Endodontics	258-451	8,000-13,000
Extraction Wisdom Tooth	194-387	6,000-12,000
2D Extraoral X-Rays	32	100

And here's the video of what they have to say about the dental care they received in Thailand.

Have a question about this chapter? A suggestion?
Email me: godfree@thailandretirementhelpers.com
I'll get back to you within 48 hours.

VISAS, WORK PERMITS

There *are* jobs in Thailand that foreigners can take. As in most countries, they must be jobs which Thais cannot perform. Immigration policy is sufficiently complex that we bring an experienced Thai lawyer to our workshops to explain it and to offer individual counseling. Happily, there are visas for almost every circumstance. We can arrange it so that you don't even have to show up for your visa hearing.

Living in Thailand: Visas and Immigration

The Thailand Immigration Bureau issues a renewable Non-Immigrant O-A visa for retirees. Here are the requirements (some of these requirements may not be necessary at your local consulate and there may be additional requirements that are unique to your area, so ask first):
- You must be 50 years of age or older.
- Have no criminal record in your country of application or in Thailand.

- Be free of leprosy, tuberculosis, drug addiction, elephantiasis, third-phase syphilis.
- Have a valid passport with at least 18 months remaining until expiration.
- The passport you hold must be the same one as the country in which you are making your visa application. British passport-holders, for example, must make their initial visa application at a Thai consulate in the UK.
- You must demonstrate proof of meeting *one* of these financial requirements:
    - A combination of Bank Balance + (Income x 12) = $26,000. (It's OK if someone just deposited $20K in your bank account). *OR,*
    - Bank statement balance of US$26,000 (800,000 Thai Baht), *OR*
    - Monthly income of at least US$2,000 (65,000 TBt).
    - Bank letter showing funds or pension statement.
- Three recent 4x5 cm. photographs (many Thai consulates waive this)
- Three completed visa application forms.
- The visa application fee is usually $250.00, though it is set by your consulate.

Before you make your application, telephone or visit your nearest Thai consulate and go over this list with them. Ask them for a copy of their current requirements and forms. Things are pretty fluid in the Thai bureaucracy so make sure that you have *current* information before lodging your application.

Once approved, your visa allows you to stay in Thailand for one year and to renew annually thereafter. You are not allowed to have employment with this visa though you may earn income derived outside Thailand from, say, an Internet business and you may change visa types if you find legal employment. You must report to Immigration at your nearest border every 90 days and verify your current address. Be sure to obtain a Re-Entry Permit at Thai Immigration at the airport or point of exit before leaving Thailand for *any* period of time.

Under certain conditions any and all of these requirements can be waived. The Thai Government is flexible and pragmatic. **Please let me know if you will need a waiver of your financial requirements and I will speak to an official for you**.

How to Make Additional Income

Once people settle in their new life the first thing they notice is how cheap travel is in Southeast Asia. AirAsia, the dominant budget airline, is always offering eye-popping specials like $20 to Vientiane, or $60 to Bali. Bali? $60? Who can resist that? And places like the Taj Mahal and the Forbidden City are only a few hours away.

If your income permits it you can hop off to these exotic destinations any time it takes your fancy. But travel involves more than just airfares and most people struggle to afford more than one trip each year.

So it's not surprising the most frequently asked question in or workshops is "What about earning some extra money for little luxuries like jaunts around this ancient and exotic part of the world?"

There is a range of options for making that little extra. And it can be "little". But workshop time is precious, and it's for *doing*, not talking. So, after talking to dozens of successful expat entrepreneurs in Thailand, I wrote a book on the subject. It's called **Making Money in Thailand: A Retiree's Guide". You can download it at Amazon.com**. Here's a partial table of contents:

> 1. BEFORE YOU LEAVE HOME: Who to talk to; what to set up in advance.
> 2. THAILAND: AN INTRODUCTION: People, places; culture, good manners.
> 3. STARTING A BUSINESS IN THAILAND:...in a very different culture.
> 4. STARTING AN INTERNET BUSINESS: Much easier. How to do it for $5.

5. INTERNET BUSINESSES YOU CAN CHOOSE: A surprising range of choices.
6. YOUR HOME-BASED BUSINESS IN THAILAND: Again, a range of choices.
7. EXPORTING FROM THAILAND: Freight, insurance, refunds, products, sources.
8. REAL-WORLD JOBS: If you've got a portable skill, chances are you can put it to use
9. BUYING OR STARTING A THAI-BASED BUSINESS
10. TEACHING ENGLISH IN THAILAND: Certification, placement, etc.

If you've already covered your living costs – and $1200/month does that comfortably – then even an extra $50/week will buy you a personal, month-long, chauffeur-driven 4wd tour of Burma, for example. Or six weeks in a seaside shack in Bali.

Wait until you're close to deciding about moving to Thailand before you buy the book. Once again, it's *Making Money in Thailand: A Retiree's Guide*. <u>You can download it at Amazon.com</u>.

Have a question about this chapter? A suggestion?
Email me: **godfree@thailandretirementhelpers.com**
I'll get back to you within 48 hours.

FOOD

If you've eaten at a Thai restaurant–and if you're reading this, I'm guessing you have–then you know what to expect. Thai food is less spicy than Indian, more so than Chinese. Above all, it's fresh. A good reason to stick with Thai food in Thailand, apart from its freshness and seasonality, is that Western food here is expensive and, generally, disappointing.

To give you an idea of how much Thais value freshness in their food, here's a picture I took at Mamia, my favorite restaurant, where I wrote this book while sitting by the river.

When I order lunch the cook sends the young woman you see in the picture to pick the greens for my meal. What's not to love about that? The meal–usually garlic chicken with vegetables in savory sauce with steamed rice–is 65 Baht ($2.20).

And to give you a feel for Thai hospitality: when I spend the entire day in a Thai coffee shop, using their Wi-Fi and drinking one cup of coffee, they are thrilled! They bring me samples of cake and glasses of ice water. If I return, they remember where I like to sit and what I like to drink. I've found this true everywhere I've been to and it continues to amaze and delight me.

Learning to Cook Thai Food

You can get ripe, sweet, non-acidic pineapple and very red watermelon year round; picked-today coconuts, passion fruit, cantaloupe, guava, grapes and oranges among many others. At 10 baht (30¢) ready to eat, they're a quick, cheap, refreshing and nutritious snack. Our workshop folk spend an entire day on an organic farm – complete with traditional Thai farmhouse – picking herbs and making Thai curries from scratch. It's pretty much everybody's favorite day, even non-cooks.

My favorite fruit treat is ripe mango served on top of sticky rice and topped with a sweetened coconut milk. The mango peeled and sliced for you on the spot is non-fibrous and you can easily cut it with the little plastic spoon that comes with each 60¢ portion.

In case you think I'm just raving about my favorite food, here's what Gene Gonzalez, a famous Filipino chef has to say about eating in Chiang Mai:

The Charms of Chiang Mai
A Chef's Tale by GENE GONZALEZ.
(The Manila Bulletin) *MANILA, Philippines* — One of our favorite getaways when we are in Thailand is Chiang Mai. The very interesting Lanna or tribal culture, the cool mountain air, and the diverse culinary offerings make it a gateway to other Northern areas. It is a destination that is filled with gastronomic secrets and discoveries. In my previous articles, I've chronicled the Sunday night market and the creative and unique items the stall owners sell that never land on the boutique and department stores.

One need not have dinner but just go through the whole street sampling the different delicacies being offered as one warms up from the chill of the evening air with food. I got around with my son Chef Gino and foodie friends, Wolfgang and Woon Hieronimi who also took us to some interesting restaurants that were being patronized by the locals with just a small sprinkling of tourists. Such restaurants are gems and keep their authenticity. It's great also to have friends who are residents of the area and have a distinct affinity with food and their culture. Here is the first of the two places they took us to.

KHAO SOI LAMDUAN FA HARM – This open air restaurant is near the famous flower market on Ton Lamyai. It is one of the oldest eating places in Chiang Mai with its old pictures and write-ups showing a very youthful Lady owner named Thong Thip (in sepia photos) who is now in her 80s. Madame Thong Thip still oversees the preparation of her famous curried noodles, the rice cakes and crackers and she does her coconut waffles on one corner of the restaurant by herself.

Anyway, *Khao Soy* or curried soup noodles is a fascinating Chiang Mai or Northern specialty as it starts with a base of rich thick curry made from pounded or stone ground fresh herbs and roots such as turmeric, galangal, young ginger, etc. As compared to a curry made with wood and seed spices, the *Khao Soy* base is fresher as it also is softer in flavors, having some secret addition to round out the heat with coconut, peanut or caramelized onion, etc. Then, this is topped with fried crispy egg noodles whereby one enjoys the first texture of crunchy fried noodles and flavors. But as the noodles soften on the broth, one enjoys an *al dente*, or to the bite second experience. A large chicken leg completes the dish. In this establishment the Khao Soy is served with chopped up pickled or salted mustard leaves.

The restaurant seems to also be a takeout center as it has several variants of rice cracker, called *Khao Tang* which is similar to our *ampao*. This is used as a vehicle for savory dips such as spiced pork with chillis or sweet coconut based syrups. What is very interesting is the *Salay*, which is a fresh water weed much like nori and sold packed. This is a crispy snack much like nori and it makes for a delicious starter.

Other items on the simple menu that we tried was th*e **Khao Kun Chin*** or northern style glutinous rice topped with pork that is either stewed or air dried like tapa. This, together with the *Khao Soy* is either washed down with sweetened tamarind juice, cold red, tart hibiscus tea or, in Gino's case, his favorite *manaw* (Thai lime) soda.

To cap our meal, we had *Khao Mak*, sweet fermented rice, quite mildly alcoholic that gives it its distinct flavors. I suppose if one had enough of these, one can get a good buzz because the rice does have some potency from the fermentation.

The best part of ending the meal was getting some freshly cooked crisp waffles made from a coconut milk base and cooked over charcoal on a very old 1930s designed waffle maker made personally by Madame Thong Thip. This is called *Khanom Rang Ping* and named after the beehive because of its corrugated shape. The crisp texture and the rich, creamy, coconut aromas just got us on the right anticipatory mood as this was our first meal in Chiang Mai.

Eating Together

Thais hate eating alone. Everyone shares food and with Thai food this works well. But if you go dining with Thais don't be surprised if they start picking things off your plate. And don't be surprised if they order dish after dish. When there is a *farang* at the table–especially when the *farang* is older and richer–your Thai guests may order a ridiculous amount of food. Don't be surprised, either, when they order dessert before eating their main meal. The norms of dining in the West don't apply in Thailand.

Getting the bill is always a struggle. Thais hate to give the impression that they want you to leave–thus giving the impression that they are inhospitable–so they will avoid your gaze until you practically tackle them to ask for the check.

When you manage to get your waiter's attention, say *Khep thang khap/khaa* (*khaa* if you're a woman). Eventually the bill arrives and, instead of $300, it's $30. So you can feel the glow of generosity without breaking your budget. Leaving the coins as a tip is usually sufficient (in Chiang Mai it elicits a grateful *wai* bow), to which you, again, simply nod solemnly and say the magic word, *khap/khaa*.

Remember: the oldest person is expected to pay the *entire* bill for these outings. As (probably) the oldest *and* as a rich *farang*, you can be sure that the buck stops with you, so grab that check and show your *nam jai*! Thailand is a foodies' paradise. And here is your essential foodies' word: *aroy–delicious.* Say it like it looks. Say it to the cook on your way out the door after a meal, with a big smile and a little bow. Trust me, the next time you eat there, you'll be warmly remembered.

Have a question about this chapter? A suggestion?
Email me: **godfree@thailandretirementhelpers.com**
I'll get back to you within 48 hours.

The Golden Fly of Love

Here is a legend that every Thai knows. It doesn't have the simple storyline or clear cut 'moral' that we expect of our myths. So turn off your mind, relax, and float downstream on this classic, baffling tale:

King Athittayawong of the City of Udon Panja had a son named Phra Suthon. One day, a brave, competent hunter named Phran Bun went to hunt at the faraway Himavanta forest. On his way, he came across seven kinnaris [half female-half bird creatures], who took off their wings and tails for a swim. The hunter used a noose to harness them and caught the youngest, Manora. He promptly brought her back to the city and presented her to Phra Suthon to become his wife.

One day, when the enemies attacked the capital city of Udon Panja the King authorized Phra Suthon to expel them. The night when Phra Suthon defeated the enemy, King Athittayawong dreamed that his intestines came out, binding the universe. He sent for an astrologer to interpret the dream. The astrologer who had wicked intentions toward Phra Suthon, deceptively predicted that it was a bad omen, for Phra Suthon had taken an evil woman from Himavanta as his wife.

To ward off the bad omen, he had to offer Manora as a sacrifice. When Manora heard of the advice, she developed a tactic for an escape.

She requested to have enough ornaments that would make her more beautiful before her death. She put on wings and a tail and then performed fabulous dances that overwhelmingly excited the audience. Then she hastily flew back to her parents at Khao Krailat. However, since Manora had been associated with human beings for quite some time, she was ordered by her father to confine herself to a palace outside the city. Only when she succeeded in getting rid of the odor of human beings, she would be brought back to the city. Phra Suthon was surprised to know what had happened to Manora when he returned to the city after his victory over his enemies. He immediately went to Khao Krailat. At the time of his arrival in the city, Manora had just completed washing herself for the total of seven years, seven months and seven days.

Thao Pathum, Manora's father, heard of Phra Suthon's arrival. The King thought that his guest had great powers and enormous tenacity so he asked Phra Suthon to demonstrate his powers until the King was happily satisfied. Then he ordered his seven daughters to sit together and asked Phra Suthon to identify Manora among the seven. If he could identify Manora, they would be allowed to get married.

Since all the seven daughters were very much alike, Phra Suthon was extremely confused. By the power of Phra Suthon's confusion transforming himself into a golden fly and landed on Manora's hair. Phra Suthon then could point her out and they got married.
–Thailand: Traits and Treasures. The National Identity Board, Royal Thai Government 2005.

Sex: The Image

No introduction to Thailand would be complete without a discussion of sex. As with most things here, it's complicated. Thailand's international image is one of wild sexual licentiousness. Along with cheap beer, sex tourism accounts for some of Thailand's appeal to single males. Sex is not a taboo or a source of embarrassment to Thais. Wealthier men commonly have mistresses and others have girlfriends of varying degrees of seriousness.

As you get to know your Thai friends better and you'll learn that having an affair is as normal as eating pie. The term *gik* or *kik* refers to the person you are having an affair with. We would call this person your lover. In Thailand being a *kik* doesn't necessarily mean you have sexual relations with them. It's more like a companion for those times when you need someone to talk to or just want to go out and have fun.

The majority of this action goes on with Thai men, whether married or single. They are much more promiscuous than Western husbands dare to be. But single Thai women often have a *kik*, though in that case the relationship will most likely be Platonic, for reasons explained below. Even here, there is considerable variation: many sophisticated, married Thai women with children enjoy outings with their *kiks* for reasons which only they can explain. And married Thai women are remarkably tolerant (by our standards) of their husbands' *kiks*. Many Thai women (and men, no doubt) carry two cel phones: one for family and business, and one for their lover(s). I wonder just how Platonic those relationships are...

Thailand's culture is one of acceptance of all aspects of life and, simultaneously, avoidance of confrontation. I hear Thai girls saying that they hate Thai men because they *nork jai,* or cheat on their wives/girlfriends. I believe that it's the culture of non-confrontation that perpetuates the *kik* custom. Let me hasten to add that, when a Thai woman *does* decide to confront her man, it's usually with a large knife in hand, and it usually ends in hospital, sometimes, the morgue. If you don't believe me, **read this article,** which discusses the alarming rate of penis-chopping in Thailand.

Sex: The Reality–Video

Thai mothers' lectures to their daughters are just like ours: nice girls finish first. Bad girls meet bad ends. Given the power of Confucian culture underlying Thai society it is hardly surprising that Western mothers would envy Thai girls' admiration for their mothers, whose advice they almost always follow.

Young Thai couples are usually celibate before marriage. I live near Chiang Mai State University and see many courting couples. Their behavior is remarkably chaste and their relationships are charming.

In general, well-reared Thai girls have no interest in foreigners, rich or otherwise. "Bar girls" are usually from poor rural backgrounds, troubled homes, or are school dropouts who drifted into the lifestyle. Having lost what reputation they have in Thai society they have little option but to try to marry a foreigner.

Since many Western women wonder how they'll fit into life in Thailand, I asked a very experienced expat retiree woman friend to talk about her experience. **Here's the video of her report.**

Marriage

There are Thai men happily married to Western women but they are rare. Western women's expectations generally clash with Thais' so the twain rarely meet.

But the behavior of Thai women is often an ideal which Western men seek but never find at home: ultra-femininity in dress and manner, apparent submissiveness, good-humored patience, and mastery of domestic skills. Their availability for marriage to Western men rises dramatically at age 30, when single Thai women are considered un-marriageable. At this point, fair-skinned (a plus in Thailand, where skin-whiteners are sold in beauty stores) males of any age with regular incomes become very acceptable mates.

Western men at our workshops who are looking for partners are introduced to a well-known, traditional marriage-broker (yes, marriage-brokers are a feature of Thai society). She grills them about their intentions and their financial position before taking them on as clients.

Have a question about this chapter? A suggestion?
Email me: godfree@thailandretirementhelpers.com
I'll get back to you within 48 hours.

LEARNING THAI

From the moment someone books a workshop–even before they get on the plane for Thailand–we start their Thai lessons.

We're pretty laid back about most of the curriculum (this *is* Thailand, after all) but learning the language is one thing we are pushy about. Here's why:

One. Most of us have comfortable life patterns and find the prospect of learning a new language daunting. Left to our own devices we might never get around to it.

Two. Living in Thailand, where few people speak English, without being able to understand anything being said or to express oneself, is like being in a silent movie. Tolerable for tourists, but not for daily life.

Three. Thais appreciate it. *Really* appreciate it. They can't wait to invite you for dinner, show you around, tell you about the kids....in other words, to include you in Thai life. Why exclude yourself from Thai life?

Four. If you have to talk to a policeman or an immigration officer and you use even a few Thai words you will find the whole meeting takes on a very friendly quality: *Hey, this person has made an effort to speak our language.*

You can now practice your Thai with a real, live Thai partner, live, on line, now, free, thanks to Skype and a wonderful site called The Mixxer. **To register and get started, go to this page and sign up for a free account.** Now you *really* have no excuse. The Mixxer matches you with someone who wants to teach Thai–for free–or who wants to swap Thai lessons for English tutoring.

Of course, your first few words may feel awkward. Don't worry; Thais are good at putting you at your ease. They'll express astonishment at your linguistic proficiency, charm, good manners, and sophistication. They'll help you learn their language so that every meeting turns into a real social encounter (and a free language lesson).

Although the little 'language lessons' in this book may seem trivial, if you learn the dozen Thai words in these chapters, you'll win hearts wherever you go. Thais who "can't speak English", for example, will be emboldened by your efforts to speak their language and suddenly start helping you in English. Your efforts can pay off in unexpected ways.

Magic Words: Nine Essential Thai Phrases

Here's some good news for the language-shy: you only need *nine phrases* to get around Thailand in style. And once you start using them and see its magical effects, you'll find it easy to add another...and another...If you watch any of the Thai movies recommended in this book you'll hear all of these phrases used repeatedly. That will help get you into the mood to try repeating them yourself.

1. ***Sawatdee***: You'll see this written *sawasdee, sawatdii* and other variations. It's a greeting and can be used to say hello, good day, good morning, good afternoon and goodbye, so it's a useful word to learn. Always say *Sawatdee* in conjunction with the polite article, *khap* or *khaa* (below). Females say *Sawatdee khaa* and males say *Sawatdee khap*.

2. Khap and Khaa: While this polite syllable has no direct English translation, 'please' and 'thank you' are two of its uses. Men say *khap* (sometimes *khrap*, but in everyday speech, *khap*) and women say *khaa*. If you listen to Thai people speak you will hear it frequently at the end of sentences. It signifies good manners and respect, so use it freely. If you are at a restaurant and you want to say 'the bill please' you would say *kep tang khap* (if you are a man) and *kep tang kaa* if you are a woman.

But how, you ask, could one word work so much magic? Well, *khap/khaa* has several functions or meanings–all of them important. For example, you can use it to mean *both* 'please' *and* 'thank you'. So if you want something you can point to it and smile and say *khaa/khap* and you will be considered both polite and knowledgeable. And if you say it to the Thai Airlines stewardess when she brings you a drink, it means 'thank you'–and she'll be charmed.

It can even be used (until you learn the correct phrases) to mean things like 'hello' and 'goodbye'. And it can be pushed to mean things like 'excuse me'. In fact, it is the WD-40 of social life: it lubricates everything. Listen for it when you're watching those Thai movies and you'll get a feel for it.

3. Sabai Dii: Another common greeting is *sabai dii*. A person may ask you '*Sabai dii mai?*' ('How are you/Are you well?'). *Khap* or *kaa* may be added on to this so you may hear '*Sabai dii mai khap/kaa?*' Respond by saying '*Sabai dii khap/ka*' ('I am well/fine thank you'). Of course you can always say '*mai sabai*' ('not well'), but then expect the follow up, '*thamay mai sabai?*' ('Why aren't you well?').

4. Khun: If you are at a restaurant and want to get the attention of the waiter or waitresses you can say '*khun khap*' or '*khun ka*'. This is very polite and will be appreciated. If you listen to Thai people calling to the waiter or waitress you will probably hear them say something entirely different. It roughly translates as, "Oh, esteemed one!"

5. *Aroy*: As I mentioned earlier, if you can tell the restaurant owner, the cook or the waitress that the food was delicious – *aroy* – you are likely to receive a warm welcome when you return. And even if it wasn't delicious, smile say '*aroy*' and don't return! Try stopping at a street stall and pointing at something you like the look of. Hand over your 10 or 20 Baht and take a bite. If it's good, smile and say '*aroy*'.

6. *Phet*: Thais are obsessed with food so the more words you can learn about food the better. (The first question they'll ask you is, "Have you eaten?" as you can't help but notice). It's also impossible to ignore the fact that Thais like their food spicy – *phet*. In fact they like it really spicy – *phet phet*. As a foreigner you won't be expected to eat some of the food that Thai people do. Don't be afraid to ask for something '*mai phet*' ('not spicy') or '*phet nit nawy*' ('a little bit spicy').

7. *Check Bin* and *Kep Tang*: Both may be used when asking to settle your bill at a bar or restaurant. It's more common to hear *check bin* in bars and *kep tang* in restaurants, but both should be understood. Don't forget your *khap* or *ka* at the end of it; '*check bin khap*' (if you are male) '*check bin ka*' (if you are female).

8. *Sanuk*: The feel good word. You'll find yourself being asked *sanuk mai*? ('Having fun? /are you enjoying yourself?'). Respond by saying *sanuk* or *sanuk mak* ('I'm having fun/really enjoying myself.')

9. *Narak* or *nalak*: cute or attractive. A woman holding a baby walks past and there are smiles all round and you say '*narak*' referring to the baby. After plenty of '*khap khun ka's*' from the mother and '*thamay phut thai dai*' ("Oh! You speak Thai?"), you're invited to join the family. The golden rule when admiring Thai children: no amount of praise, however extravagant, will embarrass their doting parents.

es' Names

When you're introduced to a Thai you will make an interesting discovery: they're introduced only by their nicknames and you will not discover their real names unless you ask. They also assume that Westerners cannot pronounce or remember long Thai names like former Thai Miss World's, Lada Engchawadechasilp.

Thais don't go by their 'real' names and are known almost exclusively by their childhood nicknames. The nickname can be preceded by *khun*, which is funny, because *khun* is a formal honorific meaning, roughly, 'esteemed'.

Of course, in formal or polite speech Thais will address each other by their given names, again preceded by khun. So Lada would be addressed at a formal event as *Khun Engchawadechasilp*. But to her friends she would be 'Lek' (little one) or her **girlhood** nickname. If we met her at a party, she would be introduced to us as Khun *Lek*-- 'Esteemed Little One'.

The chue-len (ชื่อเล่น) "play-name) is given by parents or relatives in early childhood, these nicknames are typically one syllable. They may often be nonsense words or humorous, and usually have no relation to the person's actual name. Many are Thai words for fish or chicken or bird or pig or other animals. Some use the Thai word for 'small' or 'big' or a color. They can have nicknames that mean anything. The names stay with them all their lives. One famous Prime Minister of Thailand, Plaek Phibunsongkhram, lived his entire life with the nickname "Strange", because he looked odd as a child.

Some Thais also have second nicknames given at school and usually linked with a physical feature or behavior. A boy who wears glasses may be called "Waen" (แว่น "glasses"). He may at some point adopt it as another nickname, even though he still uses his family-given nickname with family members. In other words, it is common for Thais to use *three* names: their family-given nickname, their friends-given nickname, and the name on their birth certificate.

Thai Language Books and Courses

If you're keen to get started right away, here are some of the best books on the subject:

Learn Thai – the Apps: I use this every day. It's free and you can start by learning the numbers. An excellent, convenient language tool. (And did I mention? It's free). HIGHLY RECOMMENDED!

Learn The Thai Alphabet in one Day: It allows you to master the mysterious Thai script. It's not an alphabet but an *abugida*, a writing system in which each consonant may invoke an inherent vowel sound, described as an implied 'a' or 'o'. ($12.99)

Thai for Beginners: A great learners' book for anyone who wants to learn Thai. It forms the foundation of a collection of 2-3 books that are necessary for learning any language. (Paiboon Publishing. $32.95)

Pimsleur Language Programs: Pimsleur Language Programs are well established and effective. If you're learning by listening person get the Pimsleur audio Learn Thai Language CD's. Listen before you come then, when you get to Thailand, it will all make sense. (Simon & Schuster. $120. Also used for much less $$ on Amazon).

Colloquial Thai: Covers the language that all the other books miss. Thai slang and idioms that 'official' books often miss. Surprise your Thai friends with a little slang. (Kindle. Paperback + CD: $25.95)

Improving Your Thai Pronunciation: Both a book and an audio CD that increases your ability to pronounce Thai words with more fluency. (Audio CD. $10.95)

The Lonely Planet Thai Phrasebook: The Lonely Planet Thai Phrasebook is your best Thai friend. You'll use it ~~very~~ every day. (Amazon) $9.

Have a question about this chapter? A suggestion?
Email me: godfree@thailandretirementhelpers.com
I'll get back to you within 48 hours.

GETTING AROUND

Addresses

Just to make things thoroughly humorous, Thais do not use an "address" to refer to locations. Only mail carriers do that, and they require training and a thorough knowledge of their mail route to understand postal addresses. Why? Well, for one thing, the same street number may be used more than once on a long street! So showing a Thai the written address of your destination, even if it is correct, is often useless.

Instead, Thais navigate by landmarks: "You know that vacant lot where the old repair-shop used to be...?" I have had taxi drivers who were born in Chiang Mai make several cell phone calls to my destination. Each conversation brought us closer until, with infinite good humor, I was deposited outside the door. The moral of this story is to leave plenty of time when heading to a new destination and, as always, relax.

If you're geographically challenged like me, get yourself a **Garmin Nuvi**. Every time you actually find a location you're looking, hit the button, add the name of the place, and presto! It's yours forever. The Garmin will navigate you back there automatically. To ice the cake, I'll give you the coordinates of every good spot in Chiang Mai when you get here. That'll save you many hours of head-scratching!

Transportation

Thailand offers a wonderful variety of ways of getting around. There's something to fit every budget.

Pedicabs: Pedicabs are still used in Chiang Mai and in some other parts of Thailand. Their operators tend to be older men who have been doing this all their lives and their clientele tends to be composed of dignified older ladies who have been patronizing them for years. They are slow, safe, and inexpensive. Westerners tend to be embarrassed about using them because it seems exploitive but the pedicab owners are grateful for any business, so don't be shy.

Tuk-tuks: *Tuk-tuks* are motor scooters harnessed to a two-wheeled cab. Though sometimes used by Thais for both personal transportation and hauling goods, they are mostly employed in the tourist trade. Apart from their novelty they have little to recommend them. Their drivers tend to be aggressive and to overcharge. They are uncomfortable and expose passengers to every particle of dust and pollution. In heavily touristic areas like Phuket the drivers have an even more villainous reputation and make *tuk-tuks* the least recommended form of transportation in Thailand.

Songthaews: (pronounced *song-tow*) "two rows" are the most popular form of transportation outside Bangkok, where the train system dominates. That's a *songthaews* in the picture at the beginning of this chapter. *Songthaews*–which may come in red, yellow, white, or blue, depending upon their route–are fast, flexible, and inexpensive. They can take you almost anywhere in Chiang Mai (pop. 1.6 million) for 20-30 Baht, or 70¢-$1. You flag them down from the curb and ask if they are going towards your destination. The answer is usually 'yes', so hop in the back with everyone else and off you go. Have your money (small bills or coins, please) ready so that when you reach your destination you can pay promptly and send the *Songthaew* on its way. *Songthaews* are available for all kinds of pick-ups and deliveries. For example, when my 10-speed bike needs servicing I call my favorite *Songthaew* driver who picks it up and takes it to the repair shop. Later, he'll collect it, pay for the repairs, and return it to me. Total cost for this service is around $6.

Moped and Scooters: The most popular form of personal transportation in Thailand is the moped or scooter, vehicles whose engines displace 75-125cc. Thais literally grow up on mopeds, spending the first years of their lives being carefully ferried to and from school by their mothers and grandmothers, which teaches them excellent driving habits. That's why Thai cities are extremely safe for mopeds. Automobile drivers, who grew up on them like everyone else, are very considerate of mopeds and give them right of way. We recommend them in our workshops and explain how they fit into life here. They can be rented anywhere for $100/month and purchased new for $1500. No license is necessary though, if you drive one, do carry your foreign driver's license with you since if you are given a traffic ticket the officer will confiscate the license and let you go on your way on your scooter. You reclaim your license when you pay your fine (usually $7). If you don't have your license he will chain up your bike, which can be *very* inconvenient.

Taxis: Thai taxis are metered, clean, and air-conditioned. While less common and more expensive than the indigenous forms of transport, they are the most pleasant and stress-free. Thai taxi drivers prefer to leave their meters off and to eyeball the price of a ride. This means, of course, overcharging. I recommend giving your taxi driver your destination and asking "how much?", "*an-nee-tao-rai?*", then asking that they turn on their meter before setting out (just say "meter"). The metered fare from the Chiang Mai Airport to my home, a distance of 6.3 km, or 4 miles, through the heart of the city, is 150 Baht, or $5. A typical unmetered, 'eyeball' fare is $6.

Cars: You already know this story so I won't repeat it: cars cost the same here as anywhere else.

Road Chill
Whether you drive yourself or get driven in Thailand you cannot help noticing that drivers behave differently even though traffic rules

are like ours. Though Western drivers are sometimes upset by what they see as "crazy", "dangerous" Thai driving, I think Thais are among the best drivers in the world, so allow me to say a few words in their defense. First, remember that 90% of Thai drivers came from families that did not own a car when they were growing up. Nor did they, until they were in their 30s. Thailand was not a car-culture and is only becoming one now.

Also, laws are a recent invention in Thailand. There were people living here 5,000 years before the first "law" was written. So the law is a novelty and people treat it as something that is supposed to improve their lives, not detract from it. The "law" in the Orient is understood and applied *contextually*, not absolutely. For more on this see **The Geography of Thought**. Thais don't have "rule of law"; they have "rule of law-in-context". ("Justice" has quite a different connotation, too, though outcomes are similar).

Thai drivers know the rules of the Thai Vehicle Code but they and the police interpret the Code very differently from our legalistic approach. Road rules in Thailand are applied only after the context is determined: is the road clear? (If it is, then I can ignore the red light); are there any pedestrians crossing? (then I can drive on the wrong side of the road); is that lady with two children on a moped needing to turn at the intersection? (then I'll wait before I accelerate away from the green light). If there's no oncoming traffic then it's often fine to cross a double line. If there are no pedestrians in a controlled cross-walk then the traffic simply drives through the red light.

Mopeds are given great leeway to bend the rules because of their *context*: they can't hurt anyone much in an accident. For this reason I often drive the wrong way up one-way streets without fear of police disapproval.

This easygoing attitude carries over to what in the West we call road rage. Did someone cut in front of you, or park their car in the left lane during rush hour? Well, they probably had an emergency, so just relax. *Mai pen rai.* Nobody honks. No dirty looks. Just be happy.

Seeing Thailand

One of the advantages of living in Thailand is that all of its attractions are 'home': you can just hop on a plane ($70 to most places), bus ($40), or train ($30) and you're there. We help our workshop attendees to plan–and even to book–their tours of the country. It would be crazy to come all this way and not see the world's greatest tourist country.

Tourism is Thailand's lifeblood. Visitors to the Kingdom have risen from 1 million in 1985 to 20 million today. If each visitor spends $3,000 here, then tourism accounts for $60 billion in the national economy. That's $1,000 for every Thai man, woman, and child in a country where the minimum wage is $50/week. It's a very big deal.

There are sights to satisfy every traveler's desires: beach goers head to picturesque islands off the eastern and southern coasts, while more adventurous travelers trek through hill-tribe homelands in the mountainous north.

Others explore the ancient cities of Central Thailand, where the ruins of great kingdoms now lie in silent majesty, and a testament to a glorious past. For travelers new to Southeast Asia, there is no better place to start than 'Amazing Thailand'.

Beaches. Ko Samet and Ko Chang, off the east coast, are inexpensive and easy going. Down south, Ko Samui, Ko Phangan, and Ko Tao offer a livelier brand of sun and fun with a wider array of aquatic activities. Krabi's seaside cliffs offer world-class climbing.

Hanging Out. Float down the river and watch thousands of years of history unwind before your eyes. Towns along the Mekong, including Chiang Khan and Nakhon Phanom, are unparalleled spots to relax and take in stunning natural settings. Kanchanaburi is the place to go for first-class accommodations and delicious cuisine.

Tiny, laid-back Pai, nestled in the northern highlands up the road from Chiang Mai, has a host of bubbling natural hot springs.

Hiking and Trekking. Northern Thailand offers an impressive range of affordable treks. Less-touristic Mae Hong Son and Sangkhlaburi have activities ranging from elephant excursions to river rafting.

Cultural Heritage. The temples and palaces of Bangkok and Chiang Mai, the ancient capitals of Sukhothai and Ayutthaya, and the Khmer ruins of Phimai are enthralling and accessible. Chiang Mai, of course, is not to be missed for its stunning architectural legacy and religious significance.

Nightlife. Thais are night people. They like to rise late and party far into the night. People in Bangkok, Chiang Mai, Ko Phangan, Ko Samui, and Khon Kaen hit the dance floor when the rest of the kingdom hits the hay.

Thailand's Best Retirement Cities

Bangkok (Krung Thep): with nearly 12 million people, Bangkok is Thailand's largest city and its capital. Though it's a popular location for SE Asian headquarters of some of the world's largest companies, when compared to other major world cities the cost of living in Bangkok is low.

Bangkok is a trend setter in international affairs, maintains high standards for quality of life, and hosts significant expatriate communities. Virtually every nationality on earth has residents in Bangkok.

Transportation and communications infrastructure is modern and well-maintained. Roads are good, though clogged with traffic. Health care services are world leading. Facilities for shopping, dining and nightlife are extraordinary. A futuristic and well-run international airport is easily reached by the express Sky Train.

Negatives are the traffic, air pollution, and vulnerability to flooding it was built on a flood plain and is slowly sinking. The fact that it's a *very* big city is a negative for most retirees but a positive for some.

Chiang Mai: with a population of 160,000 (about 1,600,000 in the metropolitan area) enjoys a more laid back lifestyle than Bangkok with no major sacrifices. It's the urban center of northern Thailand and is growing moderately. It attracts almost 5 million visitors a year and tourism is a vital contributor to its economy.

The city has a busy international airport, good healthcare services (12 hospitals, dental offices, spas) catering to medical tourism, universities, decent–though largely informal– transportation, a wide range of shopping opportunities from large malls to small markets, an active nightlife, and a host of other activities like adventure parks, zoos, museums, nature parks, religious/archaeological sites.

What makes Chiang Mai so appealing to expats is its location in the northern highlands (about 300 meters above sea level) that gives it an average temperature of 77F or 25C. To the credit of the city fathers, Chiang Mai has modernized without sacrificing its rich cultural history and quality that makes it unique. Central Chiang Mai, for example, is 1 mile square and bounded by a moat and remains of it ancient wall. Inside the moat is a network of charming alleyways and lanes that are ideal for wandering. But outside the moat is a well-maintained multi-lane ring road that moves traffic swiftly and efficiently

Hat Yai: near the southern Thai-Malaysian border Hat Yai has a population of 168,000 (greater metropolitan area 820,000). Hat Yai is primarily a business center that has evolved into a key transportation hub (international airport, railway, and highway) for southern Thailand.

Hat Yai is a major tourist destination for Malaysians and Singaporeans, though less so for Western tourists. As one might expect of a city of this size, hospitals, malls, markets and nightclubs abound. If you'd like to get away from the expat scene, consider living in Hat Yai.

Retirement Resort Towns

Phuket City: though Phuket City has a population of only 80,000, it's located on Phuket Island which is a major tourist destination in southern Thailand. Social amenities a good and serve the tourist market well. Housing ranges from simple to elegant and the cost of living is low compared to the West.

Its island location provides water activities ranging from snorkeling, to diving, fishing, paragliding, and a panoply of beach and marine activities. Malls, markets, restaurants, parks and nightlife are all available, though on a more limited scale as you would expect of a small island community. Medical facilities tend to cater to the medical tourist. A number of hospitals and clinics, including inexpensive Government facilities are available.

Outside Phuket City the island hinterland offers a much less crowded, even rural and laid-back lifestyle that retirees tend to enjoy. Definitely worth checking out: country living with fresh sand crab for lunch at bargain prices.

Pattaya City: Pattaya ("Pats" as it is commonly known among expats) has a population of 100,000 with a hinterland population of a million. Pattaya began to develop into resort during the Vietnam War and today has over 4 million tourists annually.

The beachfront has plentiful, albeit touristy, dining, nightlife and shopping. Jomtien Beach is the residential area where condos, bungalows and hotels dominate. Pattaya is served by rail, bus, and taxi transportation services. In addition to the usual water sports there are botanical gardens, wildlife reserves, zoos, museums, amusement parks, an aquarium, and a good range of varied activities to while away the sunny days.

The several fine hospitals catering to the medical tourism industry, coupled with the large number of expats who have settled there suggests that it is worth adding to your 'shopping list' of places to settle.

Rural Retirement Cities

Khon Kaen: Khon Kaen is a smaller city located in northeastern Thailand with a population of 125,000. It's the educational and financial center of its region. The silk industry and its associated crafts are an important part of its economy. The several universities located there guarantee a population with English language skills.

Social amenities are small-scale but adequate for a small town international retirement lifestyle. The local culture is much less commercialized than tourist cities; culturally, it feels more like the "old Thailand. Retirees seeking a simpler lifestyle with some access to social amenities will be happy here. Khon Kaen has many of the qualities of an American 'university town' (Amherst, Massachusetts comes to mind) that make it a candidate for international living.

Udon Thani: Udon Thani, pop. 245,000, is also located in Thailand's northeast. Its claim to touristic fame is its location near to the Ban Chiang archaeological site. Only recently discovered, already a UNESCO heritage site and still only partly excavated, it dates back to the Bronze Age 3,500 years ago and has produced many unique and beautiful artifacts.

As Thailand's fourth largest city, Udon Thani offers a fair range of social amenities for international living *and* is a gateway to Laos, which allows Laos-lovers to enjoy the best of Thai comforts while sampling the exotic delights of Laos.

Kanchanaburi: in western Thailand, has a population of 31,000. It is a small town with limited social amenities, small shops and shopping centers. Kanchanaburi has a memorial to the Burma Railway, of which the nearby Bridge on the River Kwai (Khwae Yai in Thai) was a part. There are a number of caves, waterfalls, temples and parks. The town would suit retirees in good health and who prefer a small rural setting. Its cost of living–for most items–is significantly below that of any of the others mentioned here.

Ko Samui: an island off Thailand's east coast, Ko Samui has a population of 52,000 and attracts over a million tourists each year–which has resulted in the development of tourist resorts and bungalows for tourists as well as homes for longer term residents. It has several small private hospitals. Even though tourism is its lifeblood, it still has the charm of an out of the way island that many retirees find irresistible, along with pretty decent social amenities.

The 10 Best Thailand Blogs

Whenever you need relief from my ramblings, turn to the men and women who explore Thailand and write about it every day. They are the intrepid bloggers, investigating remote corners of Thailand and Thai culture in ways no tourist guide could. Here are the ten best bloggers covering Thailand today, with live links in their titles:

Austin Bush Photography. A blog about food in Thailand and elsewhere. Because the author wears his heart on his sleeve (in his stomach?) it's more useful than anonymous reviews by people whose only prior experience with Thai food is from their local restaurant. A well-written food blog illustrated by a professional photographer. What more needs be said?

Thai Travel News. Richard Barrow's famous blog about Thailand, getting around, being turned on by the country, plus Thai tourism news and updates. Richard's industriousness has earned him enviable Tourism Authority press trips to tourist hot spots and advance news of interesting events. His site has something for everyone: tourists, travelers, expats, and even locals.

Bangkok Noir. An American poet in the Bangkok night world. Wonderful observations coupled with Chris Coles' own rendering of the denizens of nighttime Bangkok. This blog is not meant as a tourist guide but rather as an impressionist rendering of an exotic human menagerie. It succeeds in spades. The drawing alone are worth the visit.

Village Farang: *My Thai Village Life in Chiang Rai, Thailand.* An inspiration to travelers, country-life lovers and bloggers alike. By a professional writer and photographer, about his beloved home village in northern Thailand is one of the world's finest blogs. Its balance of aesthetics, reportage, and fluency is the envy of the blogosphere.

The Thai Pirate: *Thai Blog and Travel Stories. An Englishman's Perspective and Life and Work in the Suphanaburi Province, Thailand.* A piratical look at life in Thailand from almost every perspective. Wildly varied, beautifully photographed, and funny in a low-key, British way that makes it an addictive read.

Sevenwinds: Life on the Bookends of the World: *Living life to the fullest with Random Acts of Kindness, Generosity, and Consideration all over the World.* Bouncing between Thailand and California and places in-between. The author's enviable life is spent between California's Bay Area and Thailand, bringing fresh perspectives to both. Lively, empathetic writing and clean, crisp photographic style combine to make this one a winner.

Still Life in Moving Vehicles: *Bangkok from the Passenger's Seat.* The author is a former taxi driver who took a wrong turn and ended up as a University Professor and candid photographer. He has created one of the most idiosyncratic blogs in the history of blogdom. Funny, mordant, quirky, it's blogs like this that leaven earnest blogs like mine. Enjoy!

Jamie's Phuket Blog. More timely (today!) and more personal than any tourism guide could hope to be, Jamie's love of this beach community shines through. While highly personal, it is also well-indexed and extremely useful for anyone planning a visit. Once again, excellent photographs not only adorn the site, they reveal a great deal about Phuket and its real-life inhabitants.

Isaan Live. A blog/Internet broadcast about a north-central Thai province and its bucolic delights. This labor of local love shows what a determined blogger/broadcaster can accomplish. It has put Isaan on the map and inspired emulation and many visits to Isaan

I Am Koh Chang: *The independent Traveler's Guide to Koh Chang*. Written from and about one of the world's most beautiful islands, this is another excellent example of advocacy blogging. Once again, the elements are all here: love for the place, good writing, a keen eye, and excellent photographs. If you read this blog you will be compelled to visit.

Have a question about this chapter? A suggestion?
Email me: **godfree@thailandretirementhelpers.com**.
I'll get back to you in 48 hours.

ADVENTURE

Real Adventure in Thailand Means Real Risk

Living in a foreign culture is an adventure in itself and one of the aspects of Thai culture you'll come to enjoy is its freedom. There is more adventure available in Thailand than most people can handle. Of course, real adventure means real risk, and we come from societies that are averse to physical risk.

We like to think of ourselves as coming from "free" countries but in Thailand you will be much freer than you have ever been in your life; perhaps more free than you want to be. That freedom applies to everyone, including adventure park operators.

'Adventures' in Thailand–as in most of the world–bear no relationship to Disneyland. They involve life-threatening circumstances which require you to keep your wits about you and stay alert to risks. If anything goes wrong it will be assumed that you knew the risks involved (untrained staff, unchecked equipment, etc.) and so there is no point in trying to sue for damages. Such an idea is foreign to the culture.

Most things here are unregulated. Though there are rules on the books they are usually there to satisfy Westerners' expectations and usually ignored. Road rules, as I describe elsewhere, are generally ignored unless doing so compromises safety. Fireworks are unregulated. If you want to blow your hand off with some gigantic firecracker, go ahead! It's your hand.

Like most emerging countries, Thailand does not have a 'safety-first' culture. Deliberately dangerous activities like bungee-jumping and ballooning are even more dangerous here than they are, say, in New Zealand or France. The 'safety first' message, which was only introduced in Western countries around 1940, has not reached Thailand yet. So gear tends to be used to the point of failure, without systematic inspections, and without any regulatory oversight. After accidents there is the usual flurry of investigations and recrimination, but the underlying attitude of the culture remains *mai pen rai*: 'What can you do? It can't be helped'.

I am not writing this to discourage you from having adventures in Thailand. On the contrary. Real adventures are wonderful and life-restoring. But if you want to do something dangerous, learn about it beforehand. Get on the Internet and learn how to do a safety inspection of your gear, and then *inspect it yourself.* Watch how staff handles other people before you commit yourself to their care. Do they check girth ropes on the elephant before you clamber up into the howdah? Is the raft soundly lashed?

Another way of looking at this is that in our societies we expect government to take responsibility for us. Here, you are expected to take responsibility for yourself. If you want to get drunk and float down the rapids on a rented, cracked and scuffed inner tube then don't be too surprised if you drown because nobody except your family will be. It happens every year to young tourists and their friends are naturally upset because at home there were all kinds of safety restrictions and laws to protect them from themselves. Here, there's no legal recourse and no regulations. You are responsible for your own safety. For real.

Volunteering: Elephant Care–Video

You'll find *plenty* of opportunities for volunteering in Thailand, from caring for orphans to looking after injured gibbons. Here's one of my favorites: elephants. You can find Elephant Camp through a wonderful group, **Friends for Asia**.

Elephants need to be fed and bathed before the day visitors to sanctuaries start pouring in. Bath time is in the river, and it's pure joy for elephants. Their mahouts are a fun-loving lot and they see to it that you have as much fun as the elephants do. Just don't expect to win any water fights–their trunks are powerful watering hoses and they think it's funny to catch you off guard.

Breakfast for the elephants is usually corn and grass that you'll help cut. Elephants easily weigh three to four tons (sometimes more), and they eat around 300 pounds (136 kg.) of food every day, so it takes them a while to fill their bellies. While they're eating you'll have time to look after your own needs. The kitchen staff will have a cup of Northern Thai coffee or tea ready for you, and they'll also serve you a made-to-order breakfast.

Afternoon duties vary. I was asked to help moving equipment but I noticed, rather jealously, that the women in my volunteer group were asked to tend to one of the camp's baby elephants. Each elephant is looked after by a specific mahout, and you may be approached on an individual basis to help with training. In any event, the late afternoon and evening is when you'll have the opportunity to bond with the elephants and get to know their trainers.

Elephants have been domesticated in Asia for thousands of years but these days they're suffering from something of an unemployment problem. Since the reform of the timber industry and the advent of four-wheel drive, it's been harder finding jobs for them. Wild populations still roam a few of Thailand's national forests but, to keep numbers up, Thais have had to find new roles for their national emblem. That's where the elephant camp comes in.

Our local camp has been in business for 20 years and maintains a roster of 70 elephants and 250 employees. Tourists visit on a daily basis to interact with the elephants and watch demonstrations and the revenue funds the care of the elephants and upkeep of the facilities. By participating you make it easier for the mahouts and staff to perform their daily duties.

Beyond this, the village around the camp is home to the mahouts and their families, most of whom hail from ethnic minority villages in the countryside. There are all kinds of ways you can help out on this front, not least by teaching English in the local school. This is a great way to vary your daily routine and it adds an enriching human element to your jungle experience.

Qualifications: Other than being over age 18, volunteers do not need any special qualifications, but should be able-bodied, enjoy working outside and with animals. As in any cross-cultural context, you're asked to be flexible and be open to other people's customs and traditions.

Fees*:* Participation in the Elephant Camp Volunteer Project starts at $1295 for two weeks; additional weeks $300. Your fee includes airport pick up, accommodation, and all meals while at the Elephant Camp, transportation between Chiang Mai and the Elephant Camp, 2 day orientation, half day city tour, cultural dinner and show, onsite coordinator and 24 hour emergency assistance. **Watch this video to get an idea of life at Elephant Camp...** (Todd Cikraj at the camp told me that they've got a lady in her 80s volunteering and plenty of people in their 60s working with elephants.)

Adventure Travel

Here's a story that gives you a sense of how so much that we take for granted in the West, like trains that can climb grades, is still an adventure in Thailand. This adventure is yours for $8. You can take this train from Bangkok to Chiang Mai any time:

Adventure on Rails. *An hour out of Chiang Mai, the Bangkok-bound express ground to a halt among spindly teak trees in the hills above Lampang, and my journey southwards suddenly became Thomas the Tank Engine.*

The diesel, which had started out by growling theatrically and belching black smoke through the suburbs, had begun to wheeze asthmatically. Now it was up in the hills. So its drivers decided to give it a rest.

I stuck my head out of the window of the restaurant car in time to witness a little human comedy as the drivers clambered on to the roof while the rest of the train crew formed a human chain transferring buckets of water from the nearest trackside spring.

The diesel had overheated, so they were giving it a cold shower. The author of Thomas the Tank Engine would surely have found the scene inspirational and given it a title. But then I started to think he'd have to have a name for his main character, and given that this was Thailand, it would be long, unpronounceable and possibly salacious. "Pornpong, the diesel that wheezed" didn't sound quite right for a family audience.

There was something surreal about my immediate surroundings inside, too. The restaurant, the only non-air conditioned carriage in the train, had all its windows open to the breezes, and it was sharing its very individual soundtrack with the flora and fauna of the rainforest. In front of me a couple of off-duty policemen were studiously working their way through a half bottle of Mekhong Thai whisky and joining in on the rather salacious choruses. **Read more in The Australian.**

Construction will start next year on the new high speed railway from Bangkok to Chiang Mai. In 2016 you'll see Thailand at 300 kilometers an hour!

What Should I Pack for Thailand?

Bring as little as possible. Anything you forget you can buy here, and cheaply. Put locks on your luggage and carry as few valuables as possible. Things like passports, keys and wallets should always be secured. There are lots of clever tips on-line, but here are the basics:

Bring photocopies of your passport photo page, plus extra passport photos. Keep them *separate* from your original documents.

Make *separate* records of your passport number and all of your credit card and ATM numbers. And split up your credit and debit cards so that, if you lose your purse or wallet you'll still have access to money. ATMs here love your cards because they charge $5 per withdrawal. Always use ATM machines located in/on a bank building. The free-standing ones are vulnerable to fraud.

***Do* bring a swimming costume, a day pack, and shell-style outerwear** if you're coming in Thai winter. If you'll be here in summer, buy umbrellas and raincoats here. You'll need them and they're very cheap. I have a collection of $2 umbrellas that I've bought whenever I was caught in a downpour. Thais generally scorn umbrellas. It's much more exciting to dash between awnings and downpours when it rains!

Good quality hiking sandals and shoes are a must. If you don't have either do some research and invest in the best you can afford. Wear them for at least a week before your visit to break them in.

If you have a hobby like hiking, snorkeling, or camping, you can usually pick up gear here cheaply, especially from folks whose visits are ending and want to sell their stuff. On line research before you leave will help greatly. One of my favorite Thai classified sites is <u>**Baht & Sold**</u>. <u>**Craigslist Thailand**</u> is also good. You can look up items of interest before you leave home and plan accordingly.

Bring earplugs for the inevitable noisy hotel room or for sleeping on the bus. And toilet paper! Always carry some. Thais are generous people but miserly with toilet paper. And a good insect repellent: 25%–30% deet. Mosquitoes are not bad in Thailand thanks to our wonderful gecko lizards, but in some locations they carry diseases. The local insects prefer imported food (you) since the Thais have developed some kind of built-in insect repellent.

A spare pair of prescription glasses or contact lenses, plus a copy of your prescription, and sun glasses for the beach and bus trips. If you're coming in summer, pack everything in separate plastic bags to stop stuff from getting wet, especially when traveling on boats.

A smart phone is a great investment. They provide maps, directions, Skype for calling home, dictionaries, music, email, news, and much, much more. Aside from these, the following are essential:
- Passport with minimum 18 months validity
- Travel insurance. Some credit cards include it at no charge
- Blood donor/type card
- Details of your next of kin
- Prescriptions for any medication you require. Most pharmacists will sell medicine over the counter without a script, but it's good to be able to show your prescription to immigration.

Safety and Security–Video

Crime in Thailand is like crime in South Beach, Miami. It's largely confined to two kinds of people: tourists who come to get drunk and behave badly and crooks who come to take advantage of them. As long as you don't belong to either category, you won't encounter crime any more frequently than you do at home. And you'll be much safer walking the streets at night–man or woman–than you would be in almost any Western city. Nevertheless, it pays to be careful until you learn how things work in any environment that's new.

Here's a video of my Chiang Mai friends talking about their experience with safety and security here.

Thailand has three times the population of Australia and 20 million tourists visit every year–some of them young men who are literally looking for trouble. About 99% of crime in Thailand is between Thais. Most of the remaining 1% involves drunk or culturally insensitive tourists and usually occurs between 1-2 am. **Here's a link to a comparison between crime in Thailand and Australia.**

As an example of cultural insensitivity, there's the recent case of a wealthy British homeowner who hired a Thai crew to hang wallpaper in his new home. Wallpaper is largely unknown in Thailand and the Brit, a retired building contractor, was displeased with the result. He loudly criticized and insulted the Thai crew boss in front of his crew and refused to pay for their work.

The next day the crew boss and his brother waylaid the Brit and beat him to a pulp. He was hospitalized and will never fully recover from his injuries. The police, after investigating, declined to prosecute. In Thailand to insult someone like that is the moral and legal equivalent of grievous bodily harm so, in their judgment, the score was even. Many in the local expat community expressed concern at what they saw as police corruption or incompetence. Thais I spoke to about it had an entirely different take: the employee was, in their opinion, entirely within his rights; the insult fully justified it.

Here are some general tips from Greywolf, at **Retire Abroad.** They are applicable to newcomers to every country on earth (I well remember an Iranian immigrant to the USA telling me how he had lost his fortune not long after arriving in his adopted country: fellow-Iranians who had moved to the US before him had scammed him out of every penny):

> 'It is not possible for the typical expatriate to have 100% security. However, with a little awareness and simple adjustments to one's behavior, following a few personal safety tips may make you a harder target for the common criminal when living abroad.
>
> Living abroad places you in new and different cultural and social environments. While many of the differences will

provide exciting experiences, some of those other differences can create risks for you. These risks are less associated with higher crime rates in a foreign country – instead they are more associated with your lack of cultural and social knowledge of your new surroundings. Adopting a few personal safety tips can make your retirement abroad a safer and more enjoyable one.

We all live in a world of risks, and over time we develop an awareness and understanding of these risks. Consciously or unconsciously we internalize a set of rules that enable us to minimize our exposure to risks at home. We know which neighborhoods are safe or not. We develop mental 'profiles' of potential criminals so have a general feel for who the good guys and the bad guys are. We know when it is safe to be out and when it is not.

When you move abroad, these rules may no longer apply. The slate may be wiped completely clean and you will have to develop a new set of rules to minimize your exposure to risks. These personal safety tips can help you make an adjustment to living abroad.

At First, Trust No One: We are not recommending that you live in a permanent state of paranoia. But we are recommending that you develop your circle of friends and contacts slowly and avoid jumping into financial dealings too quickly. This safety tip applies to the locals *and* the expatriate population in your new overseas home.

The sad reality is there will be a small number of people who target new residents and tourists. Many times, they will attempt ingratiate themselves into your life. Be open to friendships but careful. Make a distinction between an acquaintance and a true friend. A smiling face from a local or a familiar accent from an expatriate is not adequate screens from the criminal element out there. Over time, let your walls down but keep in mind that if something sounds too good to be true, it is probably something you should walk away from.

Blend into the Crowd: *Be Quiet and Demure:* To the greatest extent possible, another practical safety tip is to try to blend into the crowd. Of course, depending on your retirement destination this may not be entirely possible. Nevertheless, it is still possible to 'tone it down'.

Americans have the tendency to be loud and confrontational. When living abroad, it's a good idea to get a feel for what is 'normal behavior' by the locals. Of course as your circle of friends widen, more likely than not they will feel comfortable with who you are and what you consider to be normal behavior. But there is little point in drawing more attention to yourself – particularly in public places where criminals are looking for an easy mark. An initial quiet and demure approach may be a good strategy until you get to know the lay of the land and develop confidence in your new circle of friends.

Don't Flaunt It: It is also a good idea not to flaunt your wealth when abroad. Flashing a lot of cash, wearing expensive jewelry, carrying around a big bag with cameras and laptops make you an easy mark. The risk to you is particularly great in public places where professional thieves are looking for easy targets. It's a good idea to walk around with a minimum of cash that you will need.

Don't Look Like a Tourist: In general, tourists are good targets for criminals. More often than not, tourists go home and don't press charges or follow up on investigations. Robbing tourists is one way for criminals to reduce their 'risk'. Don't help them. What does a tourist look and act like. Sit in the lobby of your hotel for a while and observe people coming and going. Vulnerable tourists have a way of standing out.

Do Look Like You Know What You're Doing: if there's anything that says 'newbie' it's how you carry yourself in public. Try to look straight ahead, have an air of confidence, and look like you know what you're doing.

Become Familiar with the Country: develop an understanding of political issues (political unrest, violence, demonstrations, elections, etc.) and economic issues in your new home. This is the framework that shapes, drives and moves the people in your residence abroad. Be aware and prepared for critical events breaking events.

Understand Mother Nature Abroad: Be familiar with the natural hazards of your country (seasonal weather conditions, earthquakes, volcanoes, flooding, landslides, etc.). If you are considering the purchase of real estate, it would probably be a good idea not to buy a home in a flood zone that has a major disaster once every ten years or so.

Become Familiar With Your City: try to develop a feel for the city or town that you live in. What are the safe and dangerous places in the city? What is the level of police protection available? How do you get emergency services? Where do the locals shop and where do the foreigners shop? Where is the best hospital? What are the major transportation networks available for your use?'

Have a question about this chapter? A suggestion?
Email me: godfree@thailandretirementhelpers.com
I'll get back to you within 48 hours.

THE DOWN SIDE

Every person, city, and country has a down side: the hidden, unacceptable aspect that locals know about but don't like to discuss. Though there is little chance that you will encounter any bad stuff, here is a summary of Thailand's down side. None of it is unique to Thailand, though it does have a local flavor. So let's clear up one thing: middle-class Thais are just like us. It's the people who have been excluded from society's progress who may pose a problem.

Good stats are hard to come by in Thailand but I've no doubt that petty crime rates are higher here than in the USA or my native Australia. Much of that has to do with the fact that Thailand is in transition from medieval serfdom (and its staggering discrepancies in wealth and income) to Western democracy, and that TV has raised the hopes of every village boy and girl (prostitution) beyond any realistic hope of fulfillment.

Also, police here function mostly in an advisory role. They consider it bad manners to ask direct questions, and they would never chase a vehicle fleeing a traffic stop as it is not part of their culture to do so. Drivers are expected to follow the commands or gestures of an officer standing by the roadside! Add to this the fact that almost all automobile drivers in Thailand started driving late in life and have no childhood experience of being driven around by parents (except on mopeds) and you have an interesting and combustible mix.

But – and this is a big but – Thailand is a free country, while ours are not. You only grasp this once you've been here a few weeks. Enjoying that freedom is a big part of life in the Kingdom. Nobody spies on you or yells at you or pushes you around. People, including cops, don't take regulations very seriously, and there's a generally carefree attitude everywhere. Cops *wei* you instead of saluting. Western law enforcement have given that up in the name of safety and I feel we've made a poor bargain.

Everyday safety, walking down the street at night, for example, is MUCH better here, too, as [this video I shot of an English couple](#) who moved here attests.

So...it's an adventure and there are attendant risks to living here. They're just different risks.

A Terrible Secret

I've served people all my adult life, so trust me when I repeat the two truths about Thai restaurant service:
    1. It's hopeless.
    2. You'll never notice.

In hospitals and places where it matters, Thais are probably the best servers in the world. But for some reason they are hopeless restaurant servers. Restaurant owners provide neither training nor supervision and appear equally clueless themselves. There are two rituals that begin and end each meal in a Thai restaurant:

The first is that servers brings you the menu then stand over you without budging while you struggle to read it and work out what you want. The notion that you might need time to decide, or a drink, is *literally* foreign to them. Thais feel that by just dropping off the menu and going away they might give the impression that they don't care about you.

Then, at the end of the meal, your server is nowhere to be found. Or if she is, you'll have to stand on your chair and wave money a call out in hopes of catching her averted gaze. Thais hate to hurry you or to give the slightest impression that you should leave. Or even that they're interested in your money. Thai hospitality overrides commercial (and even common) sense. It's wonderful and touching but can be frustrating if you've got a plane to catch.

And why won't you notice? Because they are so darn sweet and gentle that you'll stop caring.

Paper

Don't ask me why, but paper–in the form of napkins, toilet paper, etc.–is more precious than gold in Thailand. Don't leave home without it. You have been warned.

Double Pricing

I was incensed to find that I was expected to pay more than the locals for *the same damn thing*. I assumed that this was an illegal plot and that I could complain to the authorities.

I first encountered it when I went to *Wat Suthep (wat* means 'temple'), on the mountain overlooking Chiang Mai. There, right at the entrance to its sacred grounds, the saffron-clad monks had erected a sign, "ADMISSION: Thais 10 Baht; Foreigners 50 Baht". So much for complaining to the authorities! Wat Phra Kew, The Grand Palace in Bangkok, Thailand's most famous temple, is worse. Admission is free for Thais and 200 baht for foreigners!

Anyone and anything foreign is fair game for this practice. Here are some of my favorites:

Foreign Mail. If you get something from abroad you should pay a *surcharge* on the postage: anywhere from 20-200 Baht depending on its size. Needless to say, this ignores the International Universal

Postage Union Convention to which Thailand is a signatory and which binds all members to deliver each other's mail without surcharge. But rich foreigners can afford to pay a little more.

Foreign Phone Calls. Ditto. There are universal agreements about international calls, all solemnly signed in Geneva. So...my California bank publishes special toll-free-from-anywhere-in-the-world phone numbers to call. Hah! Try making an international toll-free call from Thailand: the Thai International operators suddenly lose their (otherwise excellent) ability to understand English and the Thailand Telephone Company gets to charge you its own steep international rates for a toll call. (Needless to say, low-cost or no-cost overseas calling is one of the things we cover in the workshop).

Street vendors, tuk-tuk operators, and some restaurants in tourist areas will all charge you more than they charge the locals.

If you live here you quickly work out how to avoid this practice. If you speak reasonable Thai you can ask for the Thai price or hand over the correct money. If you can read Thai you'll be able to read the Thai price because–surprise!–places where dual pricing is prevalent are amongst the few places that still use Thai numerals. Generally Thailand uses the same numerals as we do.

The good news? Even the inflated amounts are still a fraction of what you'd pay at home for the same thing. And the longer you're here the less frequently it happens, until eventually the problem disappears. In the meantime, relax and enjoy it. And further good news: a Thai drivers license gets you treated like a native.

The Ten Most Common Expat Mistakes

I think I've made every one of these mistakes so I'm listing them here in the hope that you'll be able to avoid at least some of them:

1. **Underestimating or Overestimating the Cost of Living**: The detailed budget I've included in this book is revised twice a year, so check the latest edition when figuring out your budget. Thailand's

inflation is modest and well-managed, but currency exchange values change. Do stay up to date.

2. **Living Beyond Your Means**: I made this mistake when I moved here. I spent the last of my savings living in the same lavish way as when I had a real income. Big mistake! So I suggest that you start off living on a little *less* than your plan calls for. Put the day's cash in your pocket every morning. It's kind of fun, and you've then left yourself a safety margin for things that go wrong or opportunities that come up. Here are two videos I made with local expats about their budgets and how they manage them:
Living on a Budget in Thailand and *Staying Within Your Baht Budget.* I hope you find them useful.

3. **Not Factoring in Exchange Rates & Bank Charges**: As I mentioned above, currencies fluctuate and exchange rates bounce around. Be a savvy shopper when buying Thai baht just as you are about buying anything else. Get a little exchange rate app on your computer or Smartphone and, if the Baht drops significantly consider buying next month's allocation in advance. You won't *make* money this way, but you will offset your bank charges.

4. **Trusting Every Expat You Meet**: There's a class of people in every country, church, and organization that takes advantage of new arrivals. It's called "affiliation fraud" and you may encounter it here. So, if you want to help out a fellow-countryman or woman, by all means do so. But only to the extent that you can afford to walk away and write off to experience.

5. **Not Having Domestic Bank Accounts**: Before you leave, ask your home bank for the name of their correspondent bank in Thailand. If they have one, it will make it easier to set up a link between the two and to cash checks from your home bank if you need to. Get your home bank's international banking details: SWIFT number, etc. Then open a bank account in Thailand as soon as you get here. See if you can get a break from your Thai bank on your foreign ATM charges. If you're coming to Chiang Mai I can introduce you to great bankers with excellent English–something we do for our workshoppers as well.

6. **Neglecting to Inform Tax Authorities and Insurance Companies at Home**: If you have ongoing income that may be taxable by your home authorities, talk to them now. You'll find them surprisingly helpful. If there is one thing more painful than undergoing a tax audit, it's undergoing a tax audit while you are in a foreign country!

7. **Trusting Every Thai You Meet**: Just as there are expats here who want to take advantage of your ignorance, so too are there Thais who will be happy to do the same. The Thai variety are less numerous than the Western type, and the losses you will sustain at their hands are relatively trivial. But one golden rule will save you hassle: never lend anything to a Thai that you cannot afford to lose. Thais relationship to things is different from ours. Not worse; just different.

8. **Forgetting Pension and Insurance Obligations**: If you have any ongoing contributions due for pensions or insurance policies, work out automatic payments now. It's a minor hassle to do from the comfort of your home. A major pain to do from here.

9. **Failing to Establish a Home Banking Strategy**: At least for your first few years here you will be utterly dependent upon your current, home bank. Anything that disturbs that relationship can make your life abroad miserable. I speak from the bitter experience of being unable to purchase painkillers after an accident because I did not have a duplicate debit card when I needed it! Talk your bank manager and write to every branch and department of your bank about your intentions *before* you leave home. Write emails and paper mail. Follow up with phone calls! Make sure that, when they bring up your record on their computer, your overseas residency is clearly visible, and your ATM won't be put on a fraud alert because it's suddenly being used in a foreign country–as happened to me.

10. **When Bank Cards Go Bad**: It may seem like overkill to re-state this, but believe me, it's not. The psychophysics of life decrees that, when things go bad, they do so simultaneously, in multiple dimensions. My painkiller story above? Not only did *both* my

personal *and* business ATM cards go bad, but so did my Amex card–right in the middle of a bout of excruciating pain. I spent my remaining cash on international phone calls which would drop repeatedly, just before I received a confirmation number. So: get duplicate cards for everything, and make backups of your backups.

Money and (Poor) Thais

Generalizations can be offensive and they can also be useful. These generalizations relate to something that many Westerners have not encountered because we tend to avoid poor people in our own countries and rarely interact with them when we're tourists.

When you *live* in a foreign country where many people have little or nothing then you really *are* rich. They know you're rich because you've spent a year's Thai wages just to get here--and you did it for fun! Your $1200/mo. is more than twice a local engineer's salary and you don't have to *work* for it. Remembering this makes a lot of things more forgivable.

The only Thai beggars I've seen are blind people playing music in the street. Even if they weren't playing music I'd give them money because they're poor and blind and I'm neither. The fact that they play music suggests that they want to give something back in return for our money.

Poor Thais' behavior is culturally different from that of poor people in Western countries where there are social programs to cushion them. There are no such programs in Thailand.

I have encountered similar behavior in Koreans who are culturally as different from Thais as Asians can be, and in Fijians who are geographically and culturally *much* further away. In all three cases, people borrowed from me and then kept things. And people told tall stories to get me to give them money. When I dug into this, I found that they have a completely different attitude to possessions and sharing. And a completely different attitude to (rich) foreigners than you or I might have at home if we encountered a wealthy visiting German, for example.

Thai culture is more based on relationships and contexts than ours. So if I can plausibly claim a relationship to you (if I do you a favor or claim some kind of family connection or regional affiliation) then I have a legitimate claim on your time and possessions.

I once lived in Harlem with a black family and I noticed this pattern there–and really liked it! Someone would show up and be adopted into the family and introduced around as "Aunt Emmie" and treated as a full-fledged aunt when they had no blood or marriage relationship at all. They were just in need of help.

I saw it while living in Fiji, where someone would appear at the door bearing a couple of fish on a string and claim that they were originally from the same island as you. Of course you were expected to invite them in and offer them a meal (they'd brought food, after all), then offer them a couch to sleep on. Then they'd stay. And that was that.

I suspect that the origin of this behavior is *need*. We Westerners have not known need for generations. My mother, who was born in 1912, still talks about how little they had growing up. But even in 1912 they owned a big (by contemporary Thai standards) house and horses. They were richer 100 years ago than Thais are today.

Here's a current example from my own experience: a Thai family did me a favor and asked to borrow my $1500 camera to take photographs of their daughter at the school play. They then took the camera to Bangkok. Two weeks later I was still waiting for its return.

Precautions with Money and Possessions

When poor Thais do you a favor–as opposed to engaging in a paid-for transaction–they may feel that you owe them. How you deal with that obligation is up to you. Here are some suggestions based on my own and other people's experience:

Don't leave money lying around. They've never seen money lying around and it confirms every Hollywood story: Westerners are rolling in money and don't give a damn about it.
What little *they* have goes for necessities, immediately.

After repeatedly seeing your money lying around they're likely to ask if they can have some. And you're likely to say 'yes' and start a dynamic that you will soon tire of.

Don't flash money. Don't pull out a roll of thousand Baht notes and nonchalantly peel off a few. Carry as much in your pocket as you need for the next transaction and keep the rest in your wallet or purse. Remember, we come from a society where it's impolite to discuss money. They don't.

Don't argue about money. In fact, don't argue about *anything*. There's no such thing as winning an argument in Thailand. Unless it's a significant sum and there's no possibility that you're wrong, pay up and move on. If it's a significant sum, go to the police. But do not argue! Thais do not understand arguing. It is dangerous and it will end badly for you.

Don't lend things. Give them or keep them. Or buy an equivalent item, gift-wrap it and make a big deal of the fact that it is a *gift* and not just a casual gesture that will be frequently repeated.

Politics

One of the nice things about expat life is that you're no longer emotionally involved in politics. In fact, you're usually unaware of it, which lowers your blood pressure. On the other hand, if you're thinking of living in a country it's wise to understand something of how its politics work. Thai politics is unlike our own (except for the corruption, bad-mouthing, lying, and general chicanery of course).

And Thailand's head of state is a king, which gives their politics an exotic dimension.

Thailand was, and still to some degree is, a feudal aristocracy that is making a rapid transition to democracy. The transition reads much better than it lives because, as usual, those who have held power and prestige for centuries are reluctant to give them up–with consequences that are sometimes deadly.

Here are some links to some thoughtful accounts of Thai politics. They'll give you a sense of the state of Thailand's internal affairs. The first one is by Pankaj Mishra, a superb writer and cultural observer:

Recently in Bangkok, I found myself wandering through the strange but distinctive arena for one of Asia's latest conflicts: CentralWorld, supposedly the biggest shopping mall in Southeast Asia.

Protesters supporting Thaksin Shinawatra, Thailand's wildly popular ex-Prime Minister, had set up base camp in the mall's plaza in May 2010. During a widely covered clash with security forces, they had set the building on fire, destroying much of it.

The newly renovated mall–and the traffic outside, restored to Bangkok gridlock–can project again an image of prosperity and consumption. However, Thailand itself –governed by his sister, who is now prime minister, and remote-controlled by Thaksin from Dubai–looks no more stable, or closer to being a functional democracy, than at any other time since the Asian financial crisis in 1997.

From the late 1950s onward, most Western commentators reflecting on the fate of democracy in the developing and mostly nondemocratic world shared a broad assumption: that middle and other aspiring classes created by industrial capitalism would bring about accountable and democratic governments". From *Thailand's Troubles Show Democracy's Shaky Future. By Pankaj Mishra. (Bloomberg).*

Here's a link to an excellent video and audio discussion of the struggle that has played out over the past 10 years between the feudal nobility and the Thai serfs and working people. It is produced by the Open University, UK: *The Politics of Blood: Thaksin Shinawatra*.

And, because he looms over Thai politics like a giant (or ogre, if you're a conservative) here's Thaksin Shinawatra's Wikipedia bio:

Thaksin Shinawatra: Thai pronunciation: [tʰák.sǐn tɕʰīn.nā.wát]; born 26 July 1949, is a Thai businessman and politician, who was Prime Minister of Thailand from 2001 to 2006 when he was overthrown in a military coup.

Thaksin founded Advanced Info Service, Thailand's most successful mobile phone operator, and became a billionaire. Thaksin entered politics in 1994 under Phalang Dharma Party, left the party along with many of its MPs in 1996, and founded the populist Thai Rak Thai (TRT) party in 1998.

After a historic election victory in 2001, he became prime minister, the country's first to serve a full term. Thaksin introduced a range of policies to alleviate rural poverty; highly popular, they helped reduce poverty by half in four years. He launched the country's first universal healthcare program, the 30-baht scheme, as well as a highly popular drug suppression campaign.

Thaksin embarked on a massive program of infrastructure investment, including roads, public transit, and Suvarnabhumi Airport. Nevertheless, public sector debt fell from 57% of GDP in January 2001 to 41% in September 2006.

Levels of corruption were perceived to have fallen, with Transparency International's Corruption Perceptions Index improving from 3.2 to 3.8 between 2001 and 2005. The Thai Rak Thai party won an unprecedented landslide in the 2005 general election, which had the highest voter turnout in Thai history.

The Shinawatra government faced allegations of corruption, authoritarianism, treason, conflicts of interest, acting non-diplomatically, and muzzling of the press. Thaksin was accused of tax evasion, *lèse majesté* (insulting King Bhumibol), and selling assets of Thai companies to international investors. Independent bodies, including Amnesty International, criticized Thaksin's human rights record. Thaksin was also charged for concealing his wealth during his premiership.

Protests by the People's Alliance for Democracy occurred in 2006, and on 19 September 2006 a military junta which later called itself the Council for National Security (CNS) overthrew Thaksin's government in a coup while he was abroad. The Constitutional Tribunal dissolved the Thai Rak Thai party for electoral fraud ex post facto, banning him and TRT's executives from politics for five years.

The CNS-appointed Assets Examination Committee froze Thaksin and his family's assets in Thailand, totaling 76 billion baht ($2.2 billion), claiming he had become unusually wealthy while in office. Thaksin and his wife had declared assets totaling 15.1 billion baht when he took office in 2001, although he had transferred many of his assets to his children and associates before taking office.

Thaksin returned to Thailand on 28 February 2008, after the People's Power Party, which he supported, won the post-coup elections.

But after visiting Beijing for the 2008 Summer Olympics, he did not return to hear the final Supreme Court sentence and applied for asylum in the United Kingdom. This was refused, after which he had to move about from one country to another. In October, the Thailand Supreme Court found him guilty of a conflict of interest and sentenced him in absentia to two years imprisonment.

The People's Power Party was later dissolved by the Supreme Court, but party members regrouped to form the Pheu Thai Party, which Thaksin also supported. Thaksin is a supporter, and alleged bankroller, of the United Front for Democracy against Dictatorship (aka "Red Shirts"). The Government revoked Thaksin's passport for his role in the UDD's protests during Songkran 2009. In 26 February 2010, the Supreme Court seized 46 billion baht of his frozen assets, after finding him guilty of abnormal wealth. In 2009 it was announced that Thaksin had obtained Montenegrin citizenship through that country's economic citizenship program.

Corruption

Our Western culture is a *transactional* culture lubricated by relational gestures like hugging and hand-shaking whereas Thailand's, like most Eastern cultures, is a *relational* culture that is lubricated by transactional gestures like gift-giving.

To really understand it, get a copy of **The Geography of Thought** by Richard Nisbett, which is excerpted above. Absolutely fascinating.

The fact that Easterners and Westerners *think* differently leads to massive misunderstandings. We Westerners see private citizens and officials exchanging gifts and think, "Corruption!" Well, yes and no.

Oriental officials are poorly paid compared to ours and have always been. In part, this has been a strategy of the ruling class (for whom bribes are either unnecessary because they're powerful or trivial because they're rich) to keep their taxes low and force ordinary people to bear the costs of administration. Sound familiar?

While money, usually in small amounts ($3-$10), often changes hands to facilitate the prompt filing of forms, etc., more frequently the gifts are quite literally *gifts*: elaborately wrapped gift baskets timed to the season. Displays of gifts often take up entire store departments. Most are $10-15 and an office filled with gift baskets is a source of great pride to the recipients at New Year.

Recently a Thai policewoman friend was investigating an assault which required her to question a witness. The witness was in a vulnerable situation and might have refused to cooperate. So the policewoman purchased a $14 gift basket to give to the interviewee to demonstrate her sympathy for his situation and underline the importance of the information she was seeking.

While I found this interesting, what really surprised me is that the policewoman, a single mother of two, paid for the gift *herself* out of her own meager salary. This is what I mean when I urge you to really investigate and enjoy Thai culture: it's totally unlike our own, yet it works very well. It's all around you, and it's fascinating.

Dealing with the Police

A quick summary: when you go to a police station or government office for *any* purpose:
1. Take your passport with you. Always. You will always be asked to present it.
2. Make sure your visa is valid and hasn't expired.
3. Take a Thai along with you if possible.
4. Be extremely polite. Smile, bow, and say *khap/ka*.
5. Wear clean, neat, tidy clothes.
6. *Never* be rude to a policeman in Thailand. *Ever*. The more respectful and polite you are, the more helpful they will be.

The function and role of police in Thailand is *completely different* from anything you've ever seen: they're policeman, judge, jury and–occasionally–executioner. Yet they are paid a pittance and must purchase their own equipment and even their guns.

My experiences with the police in Chiang Mai have been wonderful. They recovered my wallet, stuffed with more money than they'd earn in a month, and hunted me down to return it. Police who are dealing with Bangkok's 13 million people are dealing an entirely different set of problems, yet are unfailingly polite and patient.

As is true everywhere, it's always good to have a friend on the force. It's *especially* true in Thailand where relationships count for so much. We introduce our workshop grads to policemen and women so that they will have a relationship, in this *relationally*-based culture, established as soon as they settle here.

Also, before we get judgmental let me note that, as I write this, two of England's top police officers, each earning over $250,000 annually, are on trial for corruption.

Illegal Drugs and Underage Sex: Just Say 'No'

We tell workshop attendees that we can fix any legal problem for them–with two exceptions: hard drugs and underage sex.

If you're found with a joint on you the police will just give you a warning and send you on your way. Thailand is a civilized country after all. But anything harder than pot can get you into serious trouble.

Occasionally, for example, you'll hear about some foreigner who bought drugs from a stranger and then the police suddenly turned up and arrested him. Duh! The person he bought the drugs from tipped off the police so that, not only did he make a profit on the drug sale, he also made a profit from the tip-off money.

Anyone who gets involved with hard drugs in Thailand is taking a significant risk. And getting involved in drug *trafficking* is just crazy. Two gripping books written on the topic of Westerners caught trafficking drugs out of Thailand and who later ended up spending many years in Thailand include **The Damage Done** and **Forget You Had A Daughter**. The first is the story of an Australian man and the second the story of an Englishwoman, both of whom were caught smuggling drugs *out of* Thailand. Their stories are horrifying.

Ditto for underage sex. Only more so.

Have a question about this chapter? A suggestion?

Email me: godfree@thailandretirementhelpers.com
I'll get back to you within 48 hours.

YOUR GOVERNMENT SPEAKS

Our governments have been rescuing citizens from perilous situations for centuries. Over that time they've learned a lot about us and about how best to protect us when we go abroad. I've collected their wisdom in this appendix and, regardless of your nationality, it's *all* worth reading and the advice is worth following. Following it can make the difference between an adventure and a disaster. To make it easy, just press the link and you'll be taken straight to your government's registration page. Now you've got no excuse!

US Department of State Advice to Travelers Abroad

Though written for US citizens traveling abroad, this advice from the US Department of State is helpful to everyone. I have been a beneficiary of the State Department's help and can attest to their complete professionalism. The State Department maintains a large, well-staffed consulate in Chiang Mai. They are amazingly helpful and thorough. After someone handed in my lost wallet (with its California driver's license the only ID) to the consulate, they gave it to the police and then, after getting my local number, called me directly to make sure I'd gotten the wallet and cash back. Pretty impressive.

Sign up and register here so the State Department can better assist you in an emergency: Let us know your travel plans through the **Smart Traveler Enrollment Program**, a free online service.

This will help us contact you if there is a family emergency in the U.S., or if there is a crisis where you are traveling. In accordance with the Privacy Act, information on your welfare and whereabouts will not be released to others without your express authorization.

Sign your passport and fill in the emergency information: Make sure you have a signed, valid passport, and a visa, if required, and fill in the emergency information page of your passport.

Leave copies of itinerary and passport data page: Leave copies of your itinerary, passport data page and visas with family or friends, so you can be contacted in case of an emergency.

Check your overseas medical insurance coverage: Ask your medical insurance company if your policy applies overseas, and if it covers emergency expenses such as medical evacuation. If it does not, consider supplemental insurance.

Familiarize yourself with local conditions and laws: While in a foreign country, you are subject to its laws. **The State Department web site** has useful safety and other information about the countries you will visit.

Take precautions to avoid being a target of crime: To avoid being a target of crime, do not wear conspicuous clothing or jewelry and do not carry excessive amounts of money. Also, do not leave unattended luggage in public areas and do not accept packages from strangers.

Contact your consul in an emergency: Consular personnel at U.S. Embassies and Consulates abroad and in the U.S. are available 24 hours a day, 7 days a week, to provide emergency assistance to U.S. citizens.

Contact information for U.S. Embassies and Consulates appears on the Bureau of Consular Affairs website at http://travel.state.gov.

Also note that the Office of Overseas Citizen Services in the State Department's Bureau of Consular Affairs may be reached for assistance with emergencies at 1-888-407-4747, if calling from the U.S. or Canada, or 202-501-4444, if calling from overseas.

Australian Government Advice

Having also been the beneficiary of the Australian Government's services to overseas travelers, I highly recommend them. Friendly, helpful, expert intervention, 24 hours a day, anywhere on earth. That's hard to beat.

1. **Check the latest travel advice** for your destination and subscribe to receive free email notification each time the travel advice for your destination is updated.

2. **Take out comprehensive travel insurance** and ensure it covers you for the places you plan to visit and the things you plan to do.

3. **Sign up and register here before you leave Australia** and contact details online or at the local Australian embassy, high commission or consulate once you arrive so we can contact you in case of an emergency.

4. **Obey the laws of the country you're visiting** even if these seem harsh or unfair by Australian standards. Don't expect to be treated differently from the locals just because you're Australian.

5. Make sure that you have the right visas for the countries you are visiting or transiting and check any other entry or exit requirements.

6. Make copies of your passport details, insurance policy, travelers cherubs, visas and credit card numbers. Carry one copy in a separate place to the originals and leave a copy with someone at home.

7. Check with health professionals for information on recommended vaccinations and other health precautions. Remember that vaccinations can be an entry requirement for some countries. Also find out about taking medication overseas - certain medicines aren't allowed in some countries.

8. Make sure your passport has at least six months' validity from your planned date of return to Australia. Carry extra passport photos in case your passport is lost or stolen and you need to replace it while you're away.

9. Keep in contact with friends and family back home and give them a copy of your travel itinerary so they know where you are.

10. Check to see if you're regarded as a national of the country you plan to visit, and whether dual nationality will have any implications for your travel plans.

H.M. Government's Advice

<u>H.M. Government has an excellent travel registration and assistance program.</u> It also offers extensive advice for its citizens who become involved with crime, which is interesting. Whilst you can prepare for your travels, sometimes you can't prevent things going wrong. Here's how the Foreign and Commonwealth Office can and cannot help you:

Read the travel advice for the countries you intend to visit

Check our website for information on how we can help when things go wrong and what you should do next.

See our practical tips on staying safe and healthy and avoiding problem situations.

Follow us on Twitter, Facebook, and Foursquare to receive travel advice updates.

Going abroad? Take the British Embassy's phone number with you.

And here's where you'll find the British consul for Chiang Mai.

Have a question about this chapter? A suggestion?
Email me: godfree@thailandretirementhelpers.com
I'll get back to you within 48 hours.

BOOKS & STATISTICS

Lonely Planet Travel Guide
– by *China Williams, Mark Beadles, Celeste Brash, Alan Murphy, Brandon Presser, Tim Bower, Austin Bush.* Feb 2012. **Amazon. USD $27.99**

Publishers' blurb: 30th Anniversary edition of the market-leading guide on Thailand! For this edition our authors have hunted down the fresh, the transformed, the hot and the happening, from new transport routes to get you to the beach faster, flights through the canopy in Ko Tao and stylish sleeps for all the hip new hotels in Bangkok.

Friendly and fun-loving, exotic and tropical, cultured and historic, Thailand beams with a lustrous hue from its gaudy temples and golden beaches to the ever-comforting Thai smile. From Amazon's Customer Reviews, By Mark Colin "duke-of-urn" (Medford, MA USA) 4.0 out of 5 stars:

"Lonely Planet (LP) has introduced a new line of guidebooks, the Discover (DK) series, including this one. To me they seem similar to the DK series - lots of color photographs, less text, attractively designed, glossy paper, usually one topic per open pair of pages, but that one topic is covered quite well. Color is used for the edges of pages, to make it easy to find a section for the part of the country you are visiting. Overall the graphic design and use of color of whitespace lends both excitement and usability to the guide.

Unfortunately, there appears to be confusion about this new LP series. Although each LP Discover so far covers one country, it does NOT replace LP Country Guides. Some people have bought it thinking it is a new look for an updated country guide and are not happy with it - "This is horrible, this is like a travel advertisement, I'll never buy another LP again, etc.". Needless to say, it is not for everyone. Fortunately, you have a lot of choices in the best guide for YOU, so..."

What's Available?

There are many guides to choose from for your trip to Thailand. There are several from Lonely Planet (LP), plus there is the Rough Guide, DK, Frommers, "Travelers Tales" and "Culture Shock". Start at the library or a big bookstore and look them over briefly.

I usually prefer LP, not because it is better than Rough Guide (for some places, Rough is much better), but because LP is available for more countries. Because the style is consistent, I can quickly find what I need.

Now LP has TWO country guides for Thailand: LP Thailand (LPT) with 820 pages, and the new "LP discover Thailand" (LPDT), a.k.a. Full Color Country Guide, at 408 pages; LPT is larger but they weigh approximately the same. LPDT is comparable to DK: lots of color pictures, beautifully organized, larger type, nicer layout, heavier paper. Like DK, I think it is best for reading before you go, even before you decide WHERE to go. If your library has LPDT or DK, you might start with them, and then buy the LPT to bring with you. If you are only going to Bangkok, or the beaches and islands, LP has guides for these destinations that have even more info than LPT.

Lonely Planet Discover Thailand (LPDT) vs. **Lonely Planet Thailand** (LPT). Since LPDT has half as many pages as the standard guide, has larger type, more pictures, more white space, you would guess correctly that it does not have as much information as LPT. Mostly, it has the same KIND of information as LPT - where to go, how to get there, how to get around, where to stay, what to do, entertainment, food info, dangers, annoyances, health risks, etc - most of the basic info you need to get around. But LPDT has much less info than LPT, and it lists fewer actual locations.

I'll use Phitsanulok for comparison. It is not a primary place to visit, but I enjoyed visiting there; it is covered in both guides. LPDT has fewer than 4 pages, part of which are used for pictures; it has 1 paragraph for 1 temple and a brief mention of a few other sights, lists 5 hotels and 6 places to eat, discusses only the city, and has no city map. LPT has almost 9 pages, describes 2 wats in about one page of text, covers the city plus nearby areas in the province, includes a detailed city map, no photos, and lists 17 hotels and 11 eating options. If you had a day in Phitsanulouk, LPDT is fine. Others would prefer the additional information in LPT, to see more or have more choices. [Note: I used LPT 11ed 2005 for this comparison.]

LPDT has 46 pages for Bangkok; LPT has almost 100 (including daytrips around Bangkok). LP Bangkok has 296 pages.

LPT describes many more locations in Thailand than LPDT. LPT has 83 pages on Northeastern Thailand (Isaan); LPDT has 26. LPDT excludes Udon Thani, a mid-sized city to the north popular with ex-pats. This does not make LPDT worse, because the places that have been excluded are not primary places to visit. While choices for cutting were probably difficult, I think they chose reasonably well.

LPT has 12 pages on the history of Thailand, sections on food, and some but not many color pictures. LPDT and LPT weigh approximately the same, but I estimate that LPT has 3-4 times as much information but far fewer pictures. LPT makes compromises on the paper, pictures, type size, layout, white space, etc in order maximize the amount of useful information needed during a trip. LPDT is glossier (one reason it weighs more).

When is LPDT Useful?
For a first time traveler, especially if you have limited time or prefer fixed itineraries, LPDT (or DK) might be all you need for your trip. LPDT and DK are great for a traveler who is unfamiliar with a country; they give you a good idea of what you will see which helps you decide where to go and learn a lot quickly.

I have been to Thailand several times, but I still find LPDT useful to find parts of Thailand I have not yet visited, with pictures to help me plan which ones to visit. But I will use it at home, and bring LPT with me.

For people with middle-aged eyes, LPDT is easier to read with its larger type, whiter paper for more contrast, more white space, and color coding to navigate more quickly, though LPT isn't that bad.

Bottom Line

For me, both the LPDT and DK guides help me decide where I want to go more quickly with pictures and easier organization, but I bring LPT with me instead because it has a far more information. I prefer to travel with only a rough plan and make it up as I go, so having LPT with me is essential. It also helps when problems come up - something is closed, there is bad weather or trouble, etc.

All of the books I discussed are good, but their purposes and depth of information vary considerably. Buying the right one for YOUR needs is worth a bit of research.

A Little History

Publisher's Blurb: This lively, accessible book is the first new history of Thailand in English for two decades. Drawing on new Thai-language research, it ranges widely over political, economic, social, and cultural themes. Chris Baker and Pasuk Phongpaichit reveal how a world of mandarin nobles and unfree labor evolved into a rural society of smallholder peasants and an urban society populated mainly by migrants from Southern China. They trace how a Buddhist cosmography adapted to new ideas of time and space, and a traditional polity was transformed into a new nation-state under a strengthened monarchy. The authors cover the contests between urban nationalists, ambitious generals, communist rebels, business politicians, and social movements to control the nation-state and redefine its purpose. They describe the dramatic changes wrought by a booming economy, globalization, and the evolution of mass society. **A History of Thailand** Amazon. $24.93

The authors of this compact Cambridge University Press history of Thailand deliver on their promise. This is a vintage CUP product: balanced, full of measured opinion, error-free in typography and layout, sweeping without shallowness. There is not a better one-volume entrance to this fascinating but lesser-known South East Asian Country.

Taking the nation-state seriously, the authors show how an ethnically diverse region with formidable Chinese influence and lineage gradually took shape as the somewhat mythical 'Thai people'. Known as Siam until modern times, Thailand was an ally of the US during its Vietnam era with mixed results when the GIs arrived for R&R and even more traumatic adjustments when they took their dollars and left.

Later the hot money of the greater Asian Tigers moved here from Taiwan and Japan, only to migrate to China when cheaper labor became available to foreigners in that country.

The Thai are nothing if not survivors. Nor were they ever fully colonized, a badge of honor in a region that knew perhaps too much of European and Asian pretenders to do just that.

Vital Statistics

Population: Like several Eastern countries, Thailand uses the "house book", to count how many people live at a particular address. Since every Thai must have one, counting the population is simple. Ask where they live and they will tell you the address in their "house book". In fact they may not live anywhere near that address, but because it's a hassle, people are reluctant to change their House Book information unless they get married and start a family. If you settle here, you'll be asked to register your address for inclusion in the house book.

Thailand has 76 states and one Capital Territory, Bangkok. Here's a list of some of the major Thai cities' population:

Bangkok 10,326,093
Nakhon Ratchasima 2,582,089
Ubon Ratchathani 1,813,088
Khon Kaen 1,767,601
Chiang Mai 1,640,479
Buri Ram 1,553,765
Udon Thani 1,544,786
Nakhon Si Thammarat 1,522,561
Si Sa Ket 1,452,471
Surin 1,381,761
Songkhla 1,357,023
Chon Buri 1,316,293
Roi Et 1,309,708
Chiang Rai 1,198,218

History: Thailand is the only country in Southeast Asia never to have been colonized.

Thailand's proud history that continues to influence Thai society. You will hear and see the country's love for its King, flag, and national anthem.

Land: Thailand's diverse beauty of Thailand's landmass, from Burma in the north to Malaysia in the south, is a geographer's dream and a cartographer's nightmare. Despite the country's small size, it contains a plethora of topological features. There is no layperson's book devoted to Thailand's geography, but *this Wikipedia entry* is an excellent summary.

Demographics: Use of the word "Thai" began in the 20th century when the country shed the name "Siam" for "Thailand". "Thai" is a political and geographical designation which recognizes the numerical advantage of the Tai people, who originated in what is today Taiwan and, migrated through China, and settled the country starting in the mountainous regions, where they used their specialized agricultural knowledge relating to the use of mountain water resources for rice production. The earliest Tai settlements in Thailand were along the river valleys inside the northern border of the country. Eventually, the Tai settled the central plains of Thailand (which were covered with dense rainforest) and displaced and inter-bred with the pre-existing Austro-Asiatic population. The languages and culture of the Tai eventually came to dominate the regions of both modern-day Laos and Thailand. In more recent times, many of the Tai tribes of Laos also migrated west across the border establishing communities in Thailand. The Laotian Tai ethnic groups, often referred to as the Lao, are largely clustered in the Isaan region of Thailand. Cross-border travel and interaction between today's Thais and today's Lao are relatively smooth because there is so much overlap between the languages.

Language: Like the people themselves, the Thai language has absorbed influences over time from languages including English, Chinese, and Sanskrit while still retaining its distinctive characteristics.

Religion: Theravada Buddhism (a stripped-down, South-East Asian form of Mahayana Buddhism) may be the state religion in all but name—-the Thai Constitution requires that the reigning monarch be Buddhist, and any speech that insults Buddhism is strictly prohibited. But the ancient, native worship of the nature-spirits has survived well and is in evidence throughout Thailand, particularly in rural areas. To this mix we must add Islam, which is seen throughout the country, particularly in the south and--though not a religion in the Western sense--Confucianism.

Flora and Fauna: Thailand's diverse topology yields a wealth of plant and animal species. Intrepid visitors to the country encounter come of the world's best scuba diving, bird-watching, and trekking.

Early History: Though there are clear signs of earlier settlement, by about 2,500 BC (4,500 years ago) farmers were tiling the soil in today's Thailand, and warriors were hacking each other with bronze weapons.

Thailand Today: With annual GDP growth of 5%, Thailand is booming.

Have a question about this chapter? A suggestion?
Email me: godfree@thailandretirementhelpers.com.
I'll get back to you within 48 hours.

THANK YOU (& VIDEO)

Thanks for reading all the way through this book. If you can spare the time I'd like to know something about you. Here are some questions, along with a little 'thank-you' goodie.

If you wish you can answer these questions using the Kindle's built-in browser to access webmail like Gmail and Yahoo. You can be VERY brief as I already have the answer numbers in front of me. The questions are:

YOUR PLANS:
1. What is the biggest obstacle to your retiring overseas?
2. What is the strongest attraction for you to retire abroad?
3. What is your first goal towards retiring overseas?
4. What's your pet peeve when it comes to your retirement planning?

YOUR DECISIONS:
5. What made you decide to buy this book?
6. If you could change anything in the book, what would it be?

Here's a link to a video we shot in the grounds of Mamia, beside the River Ping, in the heart of old Chiang Mai. It's two friends of mine, John and Linda, talking about what they did before they finally made the move to Thailand.

If you have the time to give the book a helping hand, **jump onto the book's page on Amazon** and write a review. You've no idea how much authors (and Amazon and Google) value your reviews. While you're there, click on the 'Like' button and, if you already have an Amazon book list ('Listmania') do add this book to it.

If you have a financial question, like the cost of running an A/C around the clock for a month, or whether your accounting qualifications are accepted in Thailand, just ask.
Or a medical question? Since I wrote *Medical Insurance in Thailand* I've become a semi-expert on medical issues here. People ask me

obscure questions about medical care here (last week it was 'What does it cost to have a plantar wart removed by laser?' I called the hospital and found out that it's $180. So it's really no problems to answer your questions. Just ask.

And if you're starting to get serious about moving to Thailand, visit our website, **Thailand Retirement Helpers**. There's a ton of practical information there about living in The Land of Smiles. (And you can read about our workshops of course!)

Thanks again for being a player in this new global experiment: retiring in Thailand.

CONTACT US

Mail: Godfree Roberts
Mamia
64 Chiangmai-Lamphun Road
Chiang Mai 50000, Thailand
Email: godfree@thailandretirementhelpers.com
Skype: mulgagodfree
Telephone: +66-088-251-7025

DEDICATIONS

To the people of Thailand who have created a culture of happiness, tolerance, and beauty.

To my fellow-expats in Chiang Mai whose kindness and patience have made my life here a pleasure and this book possible.

ACKNOWLEDGEMENTS

CHEF GENE GONZALEZ, the Manila Bulletin

KHUN NID, Additional Photography

PAKITSILP VARAMISSARA, *Artist*

DAVE NEVRAUMONT, Finance

Made in the USA
San Bernardino, CA
06 February 2014